ROTTEN FRUIT IS FALLING DOWN

PALMETTO
PUBLISHING

Charleston, SC
www.PalmettoPublishing.com

ROTTEN FRUIT IS FALLING DOWN
Copyright © 2023 by Erin Arvizu

Hardcover ISBN: 979-8-8229-2138-2
Paperback ISBN: 979-8-8229-2139-9

ROTTEN FRUIT
is Falling Down

Because I shake the tree

Erin Arvizu

I dedicate this book to all victims of sexual abuse, especially those who were silenced. I believe you. I condemn your abusers and their enablers.

Table of Contents

Introduction

There are a lot of people involved in this story, so I thought this reference guide might be helpful. The prosecution of one individual, Sergio Anthony Delgado, has caused a great divide between good and evil. Sergio is as rotten as they come, but he didn't become evil overnight. His circus ring of liars aided him along the way. My family is breaking the cycle, so a healthy tree emerges as the toxic, dead branches fall away. In terms of this family tree, rotten individuals remain connected to Sergio, and the healing side is connected to Vinni.

The Rotten Side (Left)

Doña Ofelia—aka Abuelita

She is Sergio's great-grandmother, Felipe Sr.'s mother, and Ofelia's grandmother. She lives with her son, Felipe Sr., next door to Ofelia and her family. She loves Tweety Bird. She makes evil faces at babies and children if she dislikes them. When she makes lasagna, she bakes shrimp inside with the shells on.

Felipe Sr.—aka Senior

He is Sergio's grandfather and Ofelia's father. He showed up at the family meeting right as Felipe Jr. was leaving. He said, "Maybe they were just playing a game, and this is a big misunderstanding."

Ofelia—aka restraining order hoe

She is Sergio's mother and Tony's wife. She is also Becca's mother-in-law and Mia's grandmother. She once asked Felipe Jr. if she could have our kids' social security numbers so she could sign them up for gifts at a local church at Christmastime.

Tony

He is Sergio's father and Ofelia's husband. Also, Mia's grandfather. My daughter Luna has always been afraid of him. He thought this was funny and would intimidate her on purpose and laugh.

Gloria

She is Sergio's sister and daughter to Tony and Ofelia. She is Mia's mother. The last time I texted her was just after the family meeting. I told her not to let her kids around that fucking pervert. She never responded to me.

Sergio—aka Tonito

He is rotten fruit.

Becca

She is Sergio's wife and daughter-in-law to Tony and Ofelia. She posted a TikTok after *Roe v. Wade* was overturned implying that her husband should get a vasectomy. This is the only thing I agree with her on.

Estela

She is Sergio's sister and daughter to Tony and Ofelia. She hasn't missed one of Sergio's court dates yet. She also filed a restraining order against her cousin Trevor.

Mia

She is Sergio's niece, daughter to Gloria, and granddaughter to Ofelia and Tony. She is an innocent child who is growing up in a rotten environment. These people invited the fucking pervert to her birthday party.

The Healing Side (Right)

Carmen—aka Nana

She is Vinni's grandmother and Felipe Jr.'s mother. Her boyfriend, Poncho, has lived with her with since before I came into the picture.

Poncho—aka Grampa

He is Vinni's grandfather and like a stepfather to Felipe Jr. Vinni used to say all the time that he hated going to Nana's house. I always asked him if it was because of Nana and Grampa, and he always said, "No, I love Nana and Grampa!"

Trinny

She is Vinni's aunt. She has three kids from her first marriage: D'Aven, Trevor, and Illianna. She has been married to Denis since 2011, and together they have a daughter, Je'Nise. She is also a grandmother to Trevor's four daughters. She is very stylish and is always dressed better than me.

Denis

He is Vinni's uncle and Trinny's husband. He is from Honduras. One time I made cheesy stuffed jalapeño peppers, and he complained they were too spicy for him.

Felipe Jr.—aka Junior, Felipe

He is Vinni's father and my husband. Trinny is his sister. He loves Tom Brady almost as much as he loves me.

Erin—aka Titi

I am Vinni's mother and Felipe Jr.'s wife. Writing this book has been therapeutic for me.

Vinni—aka Vinicio

He is the hero of the family.

Olivia and Luna

They are Vinni's sisters. When I share our story, people usually ask if they were also abused by Sergio. The answer is no.

D'Aven, Trevor, Illianna, and Je'Nise

They are Vinni's cousins. We love them to pieces and it's not just because they have a pool. This is for all the white people trying to pronounce these names: D'Aven is pronounced *dee-ay-vin*. Je'Nise is pronounced *jeh-neese*.

Amore and Aliyah

Amore and Aliyah are Vinni's second cousins and two of Trevor's daughters. Kaleigh is Amore's mother and Jayda is Aliyah's mom. The Delgados doted on Jayda and Aliyah, but hated Kaleigh and Amore.

Rotten Fruit

Do you know anyone that has ever benefited from an abortion? I do. Me. Erin McKendrick Arvizu.

Before I was born, my mother had an ectopic pregnancy that required surgery. The doctor successfully removed the embryo and saved her fallopian tube, although he said there was so much scarring, she probably wouldn't be able to have children. She had suffered another ectopic pregnancy before this one that completely ruptured her other tube.

My father's grandmother, my great-grandmother, Memere Gladdis, told her she was a sinner for having an abortion. My mom asked her, "What was I supposed to do? Without the surgery, I could have died." Apparently Memere Gladdis felt that *was* the proper thing to do, to leave it up to "God's plan," whatever that may be.

Shortly after my mother had that abortion surgery, an egg miraculously traveled through her one damaged fallopian tube and implanted in the uterus. Thank you, abortion surgery, for allowing me to live. Thank you to my mother, Noreen, for not leaving it up to God.

My mother-in-law, Carmen, says things like that. It infuriates me. I was raised Catholic (sort of), but I don't participate in that religion anymore. I heard a lot of bullshit in Catholic school, but I love this one line that goes, "God helps those who help themselves." You must be proactive in order to receive life's blessings. Praying and letting things happen is not enough.

So, when my mother-in-law tells my husband to stop being so angry and "leave it up to God," it makes me feel like she's telling us to be silent and do nothing. Just let whatever happens happen. But we don't want that. We want to scream and serve justice! I feel like I've lost my shit today. It's June 29, 2022. I made my Facebook post from January 13 public for all of Facebook land to see. The meme says, "Never seek revenge. Rotten fruit falls by itself." I then posted a picture of Sergio in the comments with the words "Rotten Fruit." In terms of my family tree, there's no other way for me to describe this person.

Sergio Delgado is twenty-five years old. He is married to his wife, Becca, and they live in Gardner, Massachusetts. They had a shotgun wedding at City Hall last May, but Becca was not pregnant, thank God. I think the reason for their fast and intimate wedding was for a mortgage. Becca was in the military, and I think she was able to access better financing options being married, so off they went to tie the knot. They've been planning a big wedding reception for the summer of 2023 at the Harding Allen Estate. I wonder if Sergio will be in jail by then or if Becca will have divorced him.

Before they got married, they broke up several times. The most recent breakup was because Becca had discovered some unknown loans and mortgages on Sergio's credit report. He was unable to explain them. Sergio's sister, Estela, told me a different reason why they broke up. She said it had to do with Becca not wanting to have children. I hope Becca never has a single child with Sergio.

I've known Sergio since he was eleven years old. That's when I started dating his uncle, Felipe. I married Felipe in 2009. Sergio was almost thirteen years old at our wedding reception. At the end of the party, most of the guests had gone home, but Sergio and his family, the Delgados, were still there. My parents were there too. Everyone was helping me look for my camera. I couldn't find it anywhere. I had left it on the table where Felipe and I were sitting. All the guests at the wedding were our family and friends. Why was my camera missing? It had my honeymoon pictures from Hawaii on it. It had pictures I had just taken from the reception. We eventually gave up the search, and everyone went their separate ways, unsuccessful in locating my camera.

The next day Ofelia, Sergio's mother, called my husband, Felipe. His sister told him that Sergio "found" my camera. It's strange how Sergio was helping me search for my camera, but the whole time it was "lost" in his pocket. I remember being really pissed. This punk-ass kid stole my camera AND helped me look for it? Is he a fucking sociopath? I didn't like him or his parents, Tony and Ofelia. I had just married into this family, and I'd already figured out who I didn't trust.

My other sister-in-law, Trinny, is different. She is a kind, genuine person, and her kids are too. When I started dating Felipe, she was in the process of divorcing her first husband, Trevor. She has three children with him—D'Aven, Trevor, and Illianna. Shortly after my first daughter was born, Trinny married Denis, and they have a daughter, Je'Nise.

I've been frustrated with Trinny before. She's always running late. She coordinates things last minute. I'm a planner, and she flies chaotically, by the seat of her pants. We have disagreed on several things, including how to handle the Delgados and Carmen. At the end of the day, though, she is my family. Her family is my family. We are not perfect, but we are never intentionally hurtful or mean to each other. This is normal and healthy.

One major thing I noticed right away when I became an Arvizu is that Ofelia thinks she is the boss of everyone. She is constantly meddling, constantly gossiping, and sometimes she's flat out looking for trouble. In the past, Christmas Eve has always been a stressful occasion for me. We would celebrate with Felipe's side of the family at my mother-in-law Carmen's house.

Carmen lived on the first floor of 32 Arthur Street, which is a three decker. Ofelia and her family lived on the second floor, and Trinny's family lived on the third. My family typically arrived on Christmas Eve around five or six in the evening—whenever Felipe and I were done with work. Trinny and Ofelia would either still be out Christmas shopping or upstairs wrapping presents, otherwise not prepared to start the Christmas Eve festivities when we arrived.

Sometimes it would be eight or nine, and there still wouldn't be any food yet. Presents were not to be opened until everyone ate their food, and the rule was they were opened in age order starting with the youngest. There's a lot of people in this family, and sometimes opening presents would last until two or three in the morning. When my daughter Olivia was little, I asked Ofelia and Trinny if we could try to eat dinner by seven and open presents right after so we could get home earlier to put my daughter to bed.

Ofelia said I was ruining tradition. I said I didn't want to ruin anything, I just wanted to get home earlier to put baby Olivia to bed at a decent time. I said my family would just eat and open presents and leave when it was convenient for us, and she could open hers later with her family and everyone else. After some heated text message fighting, we finally went to Christmas Eve. Ofelia didn't say a word to my face and hugged me when she saw me. That year, Felipe kicked off the food and presents at a decent hour, and I think we left around 9:00 p.m. I know she has always hated me for that, for taking a piece of control over our family's Christmas Eve. I never ever cared about her opinion of me.

Trinny and Carmen would comment frequently about how Ofelia didn't like me. They would share stories with Felipe, and he would share them with me. I found them to be comical. I knew she hated me because she couldn't control me. Why would I even want her to like me? My kids could sense I didn't like her and understood why. I didn't keep my children from her and her family because, at the end of the day, they were family. You choose your partner, not your in-laws, right? The routine with my children was to go to Nana's house once a week. It was common for them to go upstairs to see their cousins and for their cousins, aunts, and uncles to come downstairs and see them.

I loved Mondays. One day of the week I only had to worry about dropping kids off in the morning, and then I was free to go to work and come home to an empty house. Felipe would pick up the kids on his way home and have dinner with his mom. He would text Sergio to send the kids down sometimes if they were upstairs and it was time to leave. I didn't realize this at the time, and I wish I would have, but Sergio would come downstairs to Nana's house looking for my son on a regular basis.

He would whisper into the room where the kids were watching TV and say, "Hey, Vinni, you know I play Glen on Walking Dead right? Come up to my room and see the things I got from the set." He did this quietly, so my mother-in-law would not hear. Sometimes his sisters Gloria and Estela would back up his claims and encourage my son to go see whatever cool new thing it was that Sergio had. Did Gloria and Estela know why he was luring Vinni into his room each time? Or were they just programmed to lie for him because of their family dynamic? My daughter, Olivia, was never allowed to go see Sergio's new stuff, nor was she permitted into his room where he would be with my son, with the door closed. Gloria and Estela would do Olivia's hair or nails or find other ways to entertain my daughter while my son was isolated with Sergio. Sometimes little Mia would be in the room with Sergio and my son. It perplexed my daughter as to why six-year-old Mia was allowed to be in Sergio's room but not her. Olivia was much older, at eleven years old. Mia is Gloria's child, Sergio's niece.

Sergio was in the ROTC in high school. At twenty-five years old he had dreams of becoming a police officer. He's also one of those gun-freak types and owned an arsenal of weapons— twelve guns, including the scary AK-47 kind. Being a minority and a legal gun owner with ROTC experience, he would look favorable on his police application. But these pending felony charges change everything.

I noticed through social media that Becca went on vacation to Greece with her mom and not her husband Sergio. Come to find out that's another thing felony charges affect—international vacations. If you have pending felony charges, you need permission from a judge to leave the country, and it should be for a good reason like work or a death in the family. I guess Sergio and Becca had been saving for years to go on that vacation. One day she might be grateful he was not featured in any of those beautiful pictures.

Sergio lost his guns too. Before he was arraigned in court, Felipe and Trinny each filed restraining orders against Sergio. When the police delivered the orders, they confiscated all twelve guns. This also kept him away from 32 Arthur Street. Even though he was married and living with Becca, he still made it a point to be at his grandmother's house on the days she was babysitting my kids.

The last time I brought the kids to Nana's was the Monday before Thanksgiving in 2021. Sergio came downstairs to get my son. He brought him up to the second floor to his old bedroom, which still had furniture in it, including a bed. Sergio's dad, Tony, was home too. He was watching TV in his bedroom as Sergio brought my eight-year-old child into his room and closed the door. That was his last opportunity to sexually abuse him.

The Truth

It was Monday, December 13, 2021. We had just ended quarantine. I went to my twenty-year high school reunion the day after Thanksgiving and contracted COVID-19 from an old classmate. After staying home from school and work for the allotted time, the kids and I were ready to get back to the routine, but with one small change. Carmen was babysitting my youngest while my older two kids were at school, but unlike the normal routine, I would be picking the kids up from school and picking Luna up from Carmen's to bring them to a dentist appointment.

That night around 8:30 p.m., my son came downstairs and asked if he could talk to me up in his room. I said yes and followed him upstairs. He asked me to sit on his bed, and I did. Then he blurted out, "Tonito sexually harasses me." I was in shock and horror. I asked him what exactly he meant by "sexually harasses," and he said, "He touches my private parts and makes me touch his." Stunned again, I asked when this happened for the first time. He replied, "When I was Luna's age, four." My soul died as he told me his adult cousin had been sexually abusing him routinely for four long years. I told him I was so sorry Sergio did this to him. I said I was going to report this to the police so that Sergio would go to jail. Most importantly, I told him he would never go to that house or see Sergio or any of the Delgado family ever again.

I tucked my son in and kissed him good night. Then I went downstairs and told my husband about Sergio. I announced, "We are prosecuting that motherfucker." He agreed. We just sat there silently for a while. Crying. Thinking. I googled "what do I do if my child reports sexual abuse?"

The next morning, I brought the kids to school, and then I made a plan. First, I would call my friend Reilly. She's a social worker and would know what to do. Next, I would call the pediatrician. Then I would call the police.

Reilly explained how the process would work. The pediatrician is a mandatory reporter, so once I disclosed my son's abuse to them, they would file a 51A with Department of Children and Families (DCF). DCF would follow up and then turn the case over to the District Attorney (DA). With Sergio being twenty-five years old at the time of disclosure, and my son being eight, this would be considered a criminal investigation and not a caregiver issue for DCF to pursue. DCF contacted me later that day to get some more information. Two things the woman asked me were, "Are there any other young children he might have access to? And have you talked to your other family members about this?" Yes, there were other children. Four-year-old Je'Nise lived on the third floor of 32 Arthur Street. And no, I hadn't yet told any of my in-laws about what Sergio had done.

Felipe went to his mom's house after work that night to tell her and his sister Trinny what our son had just told us. They both went white as a ghost at the horror. They sobbed. They felt terrible for my son and agreed not to say anything to the Delgados until we spoke to the police. After Felipe left his mom's, Trinny went upstairs and told her oldest son and daughter about what Sergio did to my son. Her daughter Illianna, seventeen years old, immediately burst into tears. She said, "Sergio touched me when I was little too. I was only six."

I couldn't believe he molested little Illianna when he was fourteen years old! Sergio is a predator. A monster living right inside my family, preying upon his own cousins. Trinny and I went the next day to report the sexual abuse Sergio committed against our kids to the police. We also spoke with the District Attorney's office and scheduled SANE interviews for both Vinni and Illianna. SANE stands for Sexual Assault Nurse Examiner. These people are specially trained to question sexual abuse victims. As heartbreaking as it was to know Illianna experienced this abuse too, it was comforting to know we weren't alone. We were all going to fight and heal together.

I love Illianna. I have always felt very close to her. She sleeps over my house, babysits my kids, and we have some really good conversations about her goals, her trauma, her crushes—whatever is on her teenage mind, Titi is here to listen and offer whatever advice I can. She has long curly brown hair, beautiful skin, and a radiant personality. She had a really cute prom date and looked absolutely drop-dead gorgeous in her fuchsia gown. Boys are definitely interested in her, and she wants to date more seriously, but the trauma from Sergio bubbles up.

I think back to my early sexual experiences. Although they may have felt awkward and not exactly pleasure filled, they did not trigger a trauma response. Illianna is brave, though, and is learning to advocate for herself. She told a boy she was kissing that it was too hard for her to do anything further because some things happened to her when she was younger. I was so proud of her when she told me that. I told her she would meet the right guy that didn't pressure her and would be understanding of her feelings.

Before my son came forward, Illianna had no plans of telling her family what Sergio had done to her. The incidents took place eleven years earlier, and she thought speaking up would create turmoil within the family. Worse, what if people didn't believe her? Growing up she had a conflicted relationship with the Delgados. They were cruel to her, making fun of her body. Her Tío Tony, Sergio's father, even flicked her breast as a young teenager when she started to develop. He laughed and said, "You gonna breastfeed when you get older?" Outraged, Trinny confronted his wife, Ofelia, about this.

Tony's daughter Estela barged into the conversation. Together, Ofelia and Estela minimized Illianna's experience and told Trinny, "You know how Tony is. Tony doesn't mean any harm. He just does stuff like that sometimes. It's not that big of a deal."

I always thought Tony was gross. Tony is eleven years older than Ofelia. He was twenty-seven years old when he got sixteen-year-old Ofelia pregnant. They met through Ofelia's close friend. Tony was her friend's stepfather at the time. When Ofelia got pregnant at sixteen, he left the other woman and married Ofelia. Gloria, their daughter, was born when my husband, Felipe, was only nine. At nine years old, Felipe became an uncle and gained a brother-in-law named Tony.

Once you get to know this family, you understand their dynamic. It doesn't matter what one of them has committed; they will defend their criminal as a group by lying, gaslighting, and bullying. Even if they see the crime happen before their very eyes.

The second my son told me about what Sergio had done, the entire Delgado family became dead to me. It was harder for my husband and kids to grieve this loss. It was even harder for Trinny. Trinny has lived next door to or above Ofelia and her family her entire life. Although Ofelia didn't always treat Trinny with respect and kindness, she was her sister, and she loved her. I had reached the murder dream phase already, but Trinny was still grieving her sister, her nieces, and even her nephew, Sergio, in some ways.

Trinny and I were becoming closer. We were fighting against Sergio together, and we had each other to confide in. We were both coming to terms with this predator sexually abusing our children. I don't remember exactly when Trinny called to tell me about D'Aven, but it was shortly after we heard Illianna's side of the story, maybe a week or so.

D'Aven is Trinny's oldest child. Trinny, like her sister, was a teen mom. Unlike Ofelia, Trinny's boyfriend was another teenager named Trevor. He's Black. Trinny's father and Abuelita were not accepting of that. D'Aven is a couple years younger than his cousin Gloria and did not receive the royal treatment from the family. His Nana and Tío Felipe embraced him as a child, but his grandfather and great-grandmother were not as loving. Ofelia claims she helped raise D'Aven like he was her own.

D'Aven is two years older than Sergio. He grew up with close relationships with his cousins, including Sergio. Some family members, like Trinny and Felipe, say they always knew D'Aven was gay. Others, like his younger brother Trevor, say they had no idea he was gay before he came out. I love D'Aven. He is another beautiful person in my family. He has darker skin than his siblings and is really tall. He is fierce as fuck and he loves Rhianna. He has a college degree, works two jobs, and his nails are always on point.

D'Aven's story about Sergio is different. He was not molested as a child, but an incident occurred when he was a teenager. D'Aven is now twenty-seven years old, so like Illianna, his story takes place about a decade ago. D'Aven was seventeen years old at the time and was at Ofelia's house partying with his cousins Gloria, Sergio, and Estela. They were drinking alcohol. D'Aven drank too much alcohol and went to lie down in his cousin Sergio's room. Sergio entered the room later on and sexually assaulted D'Aven.

When you are being sexually assaulted under the influence of alcohol, you remember flashes, like bits and pieces of the assault. You know it happened because your underwear/clothing is off, and the blurry memories haunt you. You convince yourself it was your fault for drinking. You are too embarrassed to tell anyone. I never told anyone about when I was raped in college until I told my husband a few years ago. D'Aven only told his best friend, Jen, about what happened with Sergio. He never told anyone else in our family. He said he was planning to take this to the grave, to preserve his family.

D'Aven filed a formal police report. Now Trinny was coming to terms with both D'Aven's and Illianna's trauma from Sergio. She had not yet spoken to her twenty-year-old son, Trevor. We all suspected he was sexually abused as well. Why would Sergio skip Trevor? What was his experience like? Like the others, Trevor was close to his cousins, too, especially Sergio. Trevor and Sergio played video games constantly and had sleepovers frequently. Trinny was hesitant in approaching Trevor with this subject matter. He had just completed drug rehab and was a young father juggling multiple kids and baby mamas.

The police told us that once they spoke with D'Aven, they were going to bring Sergio in for questioning. We didn't know how this would play out or exactly when it would happen, but we assumed Trinny would be the first to hear word that the eagle had landed. On January 11 Trinny received an incoming call from Sergio. He did not leave a voicemail, so she texted him saying she was in a meeting at work.

Come to find out, Sergio was calling Trinny to speculate about what kind of trouble Trevor might be getting into. The police asked Sergio to come down to the station, and he automatically assumed it had something to do with the bad kid in the family, Trinny's son, Trevor. Estela went down to the police station with Sergio.

When the police told him what he was accused of doing, Sergio did not have an emotional reaction. For this reason, the detective described Sergio as a sociopath or psychopath and did not describe him as your average child molester. Sergio denied molesting Vinni and Illianna and said that they were actually the inappropriate ones, not him. In response to D'Aven's accusation, Sergio admitted sexual things did happen and claimed that his father, Tony, walked in on them during the act. Tony never disclosed any of this information to Trinny. I wonder what else he has witnessed and ignored.

Once Ofelia caught wind that her precious son Sergio was accused of sexually assaulting multiple cousins, she immediately jumped to conclusions. This was all Kayleigh's fault. Ofelia fabricated an explanation that Kayleigh must have been behind this. Kayleigh marched down to the police station and filed fraudulent child sexual abuse reports against her family. Kayleigh is twenty-one years old and is the mother to my great-niece, Amore. Ofelia has always hated Trevor's baby mama Kayleigh and even took the hatred so far as to hating their daughter, baby Amore. Ofelia would make evil faces at her and ignore this baby whenever she was in her presence. Ofelia called her mother, Carmen, and told her the news. "Kayleigh is trying to ruin my family!"

Ofelia learned from Carmen that these police reports were in fact filed by her own brother and sister. Kayleigh had absolutely nothing to do with it. These were serious, truthful accusations, and her son would face the consequences. Carmen hosted a family meeting that night so that Trinny, Felipe, D'Aven, and Illianna could face Ofelia and share their truths with her. I stayed home with my children. I wanted to be there. I wanted to fight Ofelia, but it was probably best that I was not present.

Estela accompanied her mother to this family meeting. Ofelia sobbed the entire time as she was told that her son molested Illianna when she was six years old; molested Vinni routinely for four years; and that her son assaulted D'Aven too. She fell to the ground and wept. She said she wanted to commit suicide. She asked God, why did this happen? She claimed she did the best she could in raising her kids. She asked Trinny if Sergio could get treatment instead of going to jail. She asked Trinny if she went before a judge, and said she forgave him, would he get less jail time? She asked D'Aven and Illianna to text Sergio saying they forgive him.

That was all an act. Ofelia was fishing for information. She has spent every second since that moment trying to protect and defend her son, Sergio. It doesn't matter what he's done; she will lie, gaslight, and bully people out of her way or into her circus ring as needed.

Her first plan of action was to attack Trinny's son, Trevor. Pinning this on Kayleigh didn't work, but when she saw Kayleigh dropping baby Amore off to Trevor, she formulated her next move. She ran into her apartment in a fearful, dramatic fashion when she saw Trevor. He laughed and said, "You're mad your son got caught. You better stay away from my family." Ofelia went down to the courthouse with Estela the next morning, and they both filed restraining orders against him. He was served immediately and told to move out of his home, since they all reside at the same residence, 32 Arthur Street.

Felipe and Trinny filed restraining orders against Sergio because he sexually abused our children, and he is not welcome within five hundred feet of our homes and schools. Ofelia and Estela filed restraining orders against the bad kid in the family, not for protection, but to retaliate.

The Bad Kid

Without warning, Trevor packed what he could in a trash bag and vacated 32 Arthur Street, per the terms of the restraining order. He moved into my home with us. Of Trinny's kids, Trevor was the one I was the least close to. I always thought of him as a kind, sweet kid but didn't feel like I knew him well. That changed quickly when he moved in. He realized too that all the remarks Ofelia would make about me, Titi Erin, were false. I wasn't actually a terrible person. I just wasn't easy to control, so Ofelia didn't like me. Trevor was the most outspoken of Trinny's kids, and so he was disliked as well.

Ofelia and Estela loved gossiping about Trevor. Ofelia would call my husband and say, "You need to talk to Trinny about Trevor. He's doing drugs. He's messing around with Kayleigh still." She would send Carmen screenshots of all the bad stuff he was saying/doing on social media. Ofelia never seemed genuinely concerned for his well-being, just looking to spread the gossip.

Estela would do the same when she did my makeup. I hired her a few times to do my makeup for events, and she always had an update on what that bad kid was up to.

Trevor provided them with endless ammunition too. I never understood why his life was so different from the lives of his siblings until now. Trevor's dad left when he was young. Although they communicate sometimes, his father is, for the most part, absent. Trevor started smoking weed at age twelve. He got a girl pregnant at age seventeen. Now at age twenty, he has a three-year-old, a one-year-old, a three-month-old, and one more child due next month. Four daughters; two baby mamas; one stint in rehab for ecstasy and Xanax; two dismissed domestic violence charges; and a boatload of trauma buried underneath it all.

What is up with Trevor? He prefers to be mostly nocturnal, playing video games all night long. He is even taller than D'Aven and has big, curly hair. Even though he is technically a grown-up, he has a childlike spirit, and I love him for that. While he lived here with us, my youngest daughter was his best friend. He is playful and fun. He loves music, basketball and ramen. He is an inexperienced parent, but he is loving and dedicated to his girls.

It took a while, but little by little Trevor started sharing his story with me. He even calls me his therapist. He told me he sees himself in my son, Vinni. He experienced a similar abuse story to him. Trevor's abuse began around age nine and lasted until he got his own video gaming system in middle school. That's when

ERIN ARVIZU

he was able to really separate himself from Sergio's abuse. As a child he felt angry, frustrated, and sad about his dad's absence and what Sergio was doing to him. Trevor said Tony walked in on Sergio molesting him, and like with D'Aven, Tony did absolutely nothing aside from witness the crime. Sergio told Trevor it didn't matter if he told on him because no one would believe him anyway. We all know that's true now. Trevor would have been lied to, gaslit, and bullied into denial by the Delgados.

A day in the life in Trevor's childhood went something like this: He would go to school, misbehave so much his teacher would put him on red, and a call would go out to his mom. Then his mom would be pissed at him for getting in trouble at school. In between those times, he would play video games with Sergio while Sergio begged to perform sexual acts on him. For year after year. Trevor never felt he was gay. He didn't want to have these experiences with any boys or men, especially not his own cousin. I feel this has greatly affected Trevor's perception of his own sexuality. Like he feels he has to prove he is a heterosexual man by being promiscuous and having multiple children.

I've watched that show *Intervention* a bunch of times. One common theme with drug addicts is child sexual abuse and/or sexual assault. Many times these crimes create deep wounds that are suppressed and often filled with drugs. Once I knew Sergio assaulted Illianna and D'Aven, I knew he did it to Trevor. Everything becomes clearer with hindsight. Like when Vinni got in big trouble at school. Back in October, he threatened another child, and the school called Felipe to report it. I remember confronting Vinni about the altercation. He broke down crying and said his anger got the best of him, and he snapped. I asked him what he was so angry about. He couldn't tell me. He made comments in the past about how he hates going to Nana's house, and he lashed out at his siblings all the time. I knew something was up with him, and I was working on getting him a counselor to speak to, but I couldn't imagine the actual horror of what was actually happening to him. The second Vinni told me his truth, everything became clear. I knew why he was so angry and why he hated going to Nana's house.

Although three police reports were filed, the detective said we could only move forward with Vinni's case. I am considered Vinni's first person of contact—the first person he reported the abuse to. He was interviewed by the forensic interviewer, and I gave my statement to the detective. Illianna's first person of contact was her best friend, Lyanny. Lyanny also gave a statement to the detective. They said there were too many discrepancies between Illianna's interview and Lyanny's statement, so it would not be wise to move forward with a case – the defense would rip apart both of their testimonies. The detective said that since D'Aven was older than Sergio and that alcohol was involved, there really wasn't a crime that was committed—just inappropriate sexual stuff between cousins. This is completely not true because D'Aven did not consent. It's infuriating how sexual assault is routinely downplayed by authority figures, even if the perpetrator ADMITS the assault did happen and NAMES a witness. Trevor never formally reported his sexual abuse to the police. At this point, though, why should he? The system is set up for criminals, not victims.

On March 24, 2022, Sergio Delgado was arraigned in Worcester District Court for two counts of indecent assault and battery on a minor under fourteen years of age. Trevor came to court with us that day, along with a bunch of other family members to show their support. When the defense attorney entered Sergio's plea of not guilty, he pulled a Delgado move and dragged the bad kid into his speech. He said, "Sergio is here with his wife, Becca, who is college educated and works as an accountant. Sergio works full time as a masonry worker and has no prior record. I would also like to comment that his whole family is here on the other side, including his cousin Trevor. Sergio's mother and sister have restraining orders against Trevor, and he is facing domestic violence charges."

As we were leaving court, Trevor told me how Tony tried calling him just that week. Trevor didn't answer his phone. If Tony's wife and daughter are so very afraid of Trevor, why is Tony violating their own order by contacting the bad kid? I think they were hoping to provoke Trevor and catch him doing something bad, but it didn't work.

You All Need Therapy

I agree with the second-to-last thing my mother-in-law, Carmen, said to me, Vinni, and Felipe on speakerphone. She said, "You all need therapy." Felipe and I are in therapy. Vinni sees counselors at school and is in between therapists. His first one wasn't a good fit. Therapy was difficult and made Vinni feel put on the spot. We are seeking a more gentle approach, I guess. One that makes therapy feel like a positive thing and not another weekly event that's despised. I look forward to talking to my therapist, Melanie.

I think Felipe might be ready for a new therapist. He was paired with an older Hispanic gentleman who upholds some of the outdated ideals Felipe is trying to release. Instead of supporting Felipe's goals, he sometimes tries to justify this "family is blood" thing. It is not. Your family are people you love who support you and treat you with respect. Your family is not always your blood relatives if those people are toxic.

There are some major differences between mine and Felipe's childhoods. He was the youngest of four, and for most of his childhood, his Abuelita (his father's mother), lived with them. She had Felipe's dad, Felipe Sr., when she was around fifteen years old. Felipe told me Senior's father was a married man who got teenage Abuelita pregnant. Felipe Sr.'s mom is named Ofelia too. Carmen didn't have a say in naming most of her children. The firstborn was Ofelia, named after Felipe Sr.'s mother. The second daughter was Trinidad (aka Trinny), named after another family member. The third daughter was the only child Carmen named herself. Her name is Zandra. Carmen named her after her favorite soap opera star. Zandra suffered from an illness when she was little and has been blind and handicapped ever since. She lives in a residential home. Her fourth child, Carmen's only son, is my husband, Felipe Jr. Felipe's mom, sisters, and other close family members call him Junior instead of Felipe. I tried calling him Junior once, but it just felt wrong. He's Felipe to me. And since we don't have a relationship with Felipe Sr., he is our only Felipe.

One of the last times we saw Felipe Sr. was at Je'Nise's fourth birthday party. When Senior walked in, I was holding baby Amore, who was around three months old at the time. Felipe Sr. asked who each of my kids were. Vinni has long hair, so he couldn't recognize who was Olivia and who was Vinicio. I don't think he had ever met my youngest daughter, Luna, before then.

After I identified Vinni, Senior said, "Vinni, do you know who I am?"

Vinni knew who he was. He responded with "You're my dad's real dad."

Senior said, "And so that makes me your what?" Vinni just kind of looked at him and didn't respond immediately. Senior was expecting him to say the word "grandfather."

I interjected with, "That's a loaded question, isn't it Vinni?" Vinni just said yes and ran along with the kids to go play. He wasn't going to refer to him as his grandfather. He didn't know Felipe Sr. And Senior didn't know him. Vinni's grandfather is Poncho, aka Grampa. Poncho is Carmen's boyfriend who lives with her. Grampa picked up the kids from the bus stop and brought them to Nana's house each Monday. They convinced him to get McDonald's on the way home almost every time. He fixed their toys when they broke. He brought them avocados and pork rinds. He was their Grampa. Not this guy, Felipe Sr., demanding a title.

Speaking of demanding titles. Right before Felipe and I were married, we had a big housewarming party. At this party, Felipe Sr. told me I had to start calling him "Dad" once I married his son. "Calling me Felipe is disrespectful," he said.

There was no fucking way I would ever refer to this pendejo as "Dad" so I just responded with "Maybe I just won't call you." I guess sarcastic remarks are a defense mechanism I use when dealing with disrespectful men. I learned it from my mother,

Noreen. I was allowed to express my opinions as a child. At the end of the day, I had to eat what was served for dinner, do chores, be nice to my brother, and follow my parents' rules, but I could say when I felt something was dumb, and I could disagree with my parents about something without severe punishment. Felipe's family didn't communicate this freely. One of his defense mechanisms is to shut up and retreat until the fire settles down. Trevor does this too.

I'm the fire in this house. I get angry and explosive when everything feels one sided. So when I feel upset about something and Felipe retreats instead of saying his side, my fire grows. This also happened with Carmen. I exploded on her. I received zero communication from her since January. To me, it felt like she didn't care enough about our relationship to say anything. I do love Carmen and miss her as my mother-in-law, but she refuses to break the cycle.

You don't understand the breadth of the toll sexual abuse takes on a family until you're experiencing it firsthand. On the surface you see child victims and the predator. Just below that you see the family dynamic and understand how the abuse cycle perpetuated. You see who protects the victims and who protects the predators. For us, it was a great divide.

It was normal for Ofelia to have coffee with her mother since she lived right upstairs and didn't work. It was a few weeks after the kids stopped going to Carmen's, but before the police had questioned Sergio. We were all walking on eggshells waiting for the other foot to drop. It was a Monday, and Ofelia went downstairs to have coffee with Carmen. Ofelia noticed that our kids hadn't been coming to Nana's house lately and made a comment. Carmen said something like "Yeah, they were sick so have been staying home." COVID-19 was a good excuse for maintaining distance with family members during this interim time. After Ofelia asked about my kids, her phone rang, and it was Sergio. He just so happened to call while Ofelia was with his Nana on a Monday. Sergio was at work.

He asked to talk to Nana, and I wonder if he was listening for Luna in the background, trying to figure out whether or not he'd have access to Vinni that day. It had been a long time since he saw him. Vinni told me one time Ofelia knocked on Sergio's door while Vinni was in there with him. Why was it normal for Sergio to be behind a closed door with my son?

It was normal for the Delgados to cross boundaries, and it was normal for me to be pissed about it and fire back. They would always want to take my kids places but wouldn't put them in car seats. This was a big safety issue for me, and I told everybody, Ofelia does not take my kids anywhere if there are no car seats.

When Olivia was a small girl, she casually said to me one day, "Mom, it hurts so bad when you wax your legs, right?" I asked her how she knew what it felt like, and she said, "Titi Ofelia waxed my legs." When we asked Ofelia why the fuck she waxed our seven-year-old's legs, she said Olivia asked her to do it, so she did.

Another time Olivia told me that Gloria, Sergio's sister, breastfed my daughter Luna. I texted Gloria, asking if this was true, and she said, "Yes. Are you mad?" I responded kindly because at the time I considered her my niece. I did not think of Gloria as a truly genuine person, but I didn't hate her. I told her breastfeeding is something I only want me and Luna to do. It was my special bond with my baby that I didn't want to share with her. Her daughter Mia was two years old at the time and still nursing. Luna was an infant, and she had not run out of my pumped breastmilk that day. Carmen even had a can of formula as backup food too. Gloria breastfed my baby solely because she was lactating and had access to her.

Ofelia and Tony also committed financial abuse routinely. I've heard countless examples from family members. Even my husband, Felipe, has one. When he was younger, he worked for Tony at one of his masonry jobs and worked a bunch of hours. When Felipe received his paycheck, it was short based on the agreed-upon wage and the hours he worked. He confronted Ofelia, who was in charge of doing the books. She reacted defensively, insisting he was paid correctly, and refused to give him any more money. Felipe can be stubborn as fuck, and so he held his ground and stopped speaking to his sister. He knew since he was little that Ofelia was not a trustworthy person.

Ofelia kept trying to creep her way back into Felipe's life, but he ignored her attempts. She even called him crying one day because her car had broken down. She was begging Felipe to fix it for her. He said no. A few months later, she gave him a birthday card with a big "I'm sorry" note in it. He showed it to his mom, and she told him he should forgive Ofelia. "She's your sister," she said. "She's your family." He did eventually forgive Ofelia, but he never forgot.

They scammed Poncho too. They borrowed a bunch of money from him to buy a house, but the deal never came together. They never moved, never bought an actual house, and Poncho was out thousands of dollars.

Another time Ofelia said she was going to take Carmen to Israel, the Holy Land, as a Christmas gift and expected Trinny and I each to give her hundreds of dollars toward her and Carmen's tickets. I said no. I'm sure I was to blame as to why the trip never came to fruition, but no way in fuck I trusted her not to scam me. Trinny gave her money toward that trip, and I hope she got it back, but knowing Ofelia, I'm skeptical.

Each Delgado family member displays narcissistic/sociopathic tendencies in their own ways. Sergio is obviously the worst. He molests children and hurts animals. Vinni told me a story once about Sergio murdering a squirrel in front of him. Tony and Ofelia are the worst too; they enabled his abuse to continue for more than a decade, affecting multiple victims. They saw the abuse happen with their own eyes and did nothing.

They continue to protect and defend Sergio, perpetuating the abuse cycle.

When Vinni told me that Mia would be in the room with him and Sergio sometimes, my heart sank again. Even though Mia was no longer my niece, I did not want her to be abused by her gross uncle. She's only six years old, the same age when it happened to Illianna. Why would Sergio allow her to be in the room? Vinni explained that she would be sitting on the floor watching TV or otherwise not paying attention to what Sergio was doing to him. Was she desensitized to it? Was she being groomed to think this was normal? Was she just waiting her turn, and Sergio molested her after Vinni left? Until we hear Mia's side of the story, we won't know for sure. As soon as my children revealed that Mia was potentially being abused, I reported this fact to DCF and filed a 51A. I assume this case was then handed to the DA to investigate since she too is a minor, but DCF doesn't give you any follow-up after you report something to them. I do wish that Gloria took these accusations more seriously, for her own daughter's sake.

Carmen never meant for any harm to happen to my son or Trinny's kids, but she was unable to stop Sergio because his parents and siblings enabled him. In order to break the cycle, we have to stop enablers. They can't exist in our family because they are untrustworthy and allow children to be abused.

I think Carmen could use some therapy to help her understand just how unhealthy her own relationship with her daughter Ofelia really is. Until then, I won't be calling Carmen, per her wishes. That was the very last thing she said to us that day on speakerphone. She said, "Don't ever call this number again."

The Circus

I never doubted my son's truth for a single second. He had absolutely nothing to gain by coming forward with his abuse, besides from making it stop. It's common for adults to second-guess children. Imagine how many parents hear their children report acts of sexual abuse only for them to respond with "So-and-so is a good person. They would never do anything like that. Why are you saying such crazy things?"

Vinni had no idea how deep Pandora's box would be once he disclosed his sexual abuse. He could never have wrapped his head around what this would mean for our family structure or how quickly things would change. In early 2022, Carmen hired a realtor to sell that three decker. She sold that house, and both Carmen and Trinny purchased new homes. The only people living at 32 Arthur Street now are the Delgados, and their rent just doubled under the new owners.

Trinny and her family have no contact with the Delgados. They know how abusive and evil these people are, and they are happily focused on celebrating their new beginnings in peace. Carmen has decided that since Ofelia is her daughter, she will not disown her no matter what. No matter how many crimes Ofelia commits, she is her daughter and she is forever her family. This is that toxic "family is blood" thing I can't stand.

The Delgados lost about a dozen family members between my and Trinny's family. They have gone from a big group to scrounging up whatever relatives they can muster. This explains their circus mates at court each month. At Sergio's restraining order hearing, he was accompanied by Ofelia, Estela, and his attorney. We later found out Becca was getting a nose job that day. It made me happy to know she spent $15,000 on her face and that that money was not available for Sergio's defense attorney.

At Sergio's arraignment, Becca and her mother were at court, alongside his attorney, Ofelia, and Estela. The first pretrial conference hearing had an interesting assortment of Sergio supporters. Becca, Ofelia, and Estela were there—the usual players—but then we noticed Felipe Sr., Maria, and Angel too.

Felipe Sr. was never faithful to Carmen during their marriage. He had a longtime girlfriend named Charlene and had relations with another woman named Maria. Maria was a very close family friend who even lived with them during periods of time. Even after she moved into her own place, she remained close friends with Carmen. Maria became pregnant at one point, and Carmen was by her side at the hospital, supporting her while she gave birth. Maria named her son Angel.

Everybody asked Maria who Angel's father was, but she always said it was someone you didn't know, or someone else. There was never a clear answer. Felipe Sr.'s mother, Abuelita, felt bad for Maria and her son Angel. She would take them out shopping and out to eat frequently.

As Angel grew up, everyone noticed the strong resemblance to Felipe Sr. Senior took a DNA test when Angel was around nine or ten years old, and turns out Felipe Sr. is 99.9 percent Angel's father. As soon as the news was clear, Felipe Sr. and his mother disowned Angel. He did not want this child to be his son and griped about paying child support. Felipe Sr. and Carmen eventually divorced when my husband was around nineteen years old. They were already divorced when Felipe Sr. found out Angel was his son. Carmen remained friends with Maria. Ofelia was mad at Abuelita and her father for disowning Angel. She started bringing him to her house and to family functions to continue spending time with him.

Angel resented Felipe Sr. as a young adolescent and teenager. Felipe Sr. would boss him around when he saw him but was not a loving father who wanted a relationship with him. Angel is in his early twenties now. When Felipe told his mom he saw Maria and Angel at court with Sergio, Carmen said, "That explains why Maria stopped talking to me." I wonder what strict orders they received from Ofelia.

Maria suffers from diabetes and lost a foot to the disease not too long ago. She was in and out of the hospital for a period of time and listed Ofelia as her daughter on her hospital forms when she had surgery. This was confusing for Ofelia at times because the hospital would call her and be like "Your mom has been admitted to the hospital again." And she would have to think, "Is this my real mother or the one I lie about and say is my mother?"

Honestly, it must be exhausting to lie as much as Ofelia does. I wonder what version of the story she shared with Maria and Angel to convince them that they should support her son at court who is facing child molestation charges. I also wonder about Angel. He is a few years younger than Sergio and used to spend a lot of time at Ofelia's house as a child. Did Sergio ever do anything to him?

Next let's talk about Becca, Sergio's wife. She reminds me of myself in some ways. She's a twenty-six-year-old white girl who works as an accountant and is newly married to a Hispanic husband. She is very pretty and on the surface, she is quite smart. She served in the military, holds a bachelor's and master's degree, and is studying for the CPA exam. She has a good job working at an accounting firm. Like Becca, I am also a white girl who married a Hispanic guy at age twenty-six, and I've worked as an accountant for sixteen years. Our biggest difference is I'm more mature and wiser beyond words compared to Becca.

If someone accused my husband of sexual abuse or sexual assault, I would investigate the shit out of these claims before coming to my conclusions. As much as I love Felipe, or any person for that matter, I would never completely disregard serious allegations such as this without first gathering all the facts. When we first filed the restraining orders against Sergio, I messaged Becca on Facebook. I felt bad for her. Here she was, this young girl, without any clue as to how fucked up of a person her husband really is. I knew she was not being told the full story. No Delgado ever tells the full story.

After the detective questioned Sergio about his sexual abuse accusations, he asked Sergio what he was going to say to his wife when he got home. Sergio's response: "I don't know." I think that's extremely interesting, like he had to come up with a plan. Telling the truth doesn't require an elaborate plan.

Becca and Sergio tied the knot at City Hall on May 6, 2021. Ofelia and the family were present and are documented in Becca's wedding photos, but not a single one of her new in-laws acknowledged or publicly celebrated their wedding. Ofelia, Gloria and Estela made fun of Becca constantly, saying her feet stunk and she was no good for Sergio. Becca used to complain to Trinny and D'Aven about how toxic her mother-in-law and new sisters-in-law were.

Becca met Sergio through his aunt Trinny. Trinny and Becca worked together at Baystate Bank and were friends. Becca started talking to Sergio at Trinny's baby shower when she was pregnant with Je'Nise. The rest is history, I guess.

Becca and Sergio own a home in Gardner, Massachusetts. They purchased it for $250,000, and there are five schools within a two-and-a-half-mile radius of their home. I wonder if this will be allowed once he has to register as a sex offender. MCI maximum prison is not too far from there. I wonder if this is the facility Sergio will end up at once he's convicted. I also wonder how much longer Becca will choose to be blindfolded. When will she see her husband's true colors and divorce his ass?

Ofelia continues to mock us on social media. She says things like "Another one joins the circus." "Bozo and the clowns are at it again." I saw something this morning on TikTok. An experienced therapist said that if an innocent man is accused of abusing his wife, he will usually respond in a very concerned fashion. He will ask, "What happened to my wife?" and "Why do you think I'm hurting her?" If an abusive man is accused of abusing his wife, he will usually respond aggressively, denying the claims and attacking his accusers. I think this is true for child abusers too. The first thing they do when you expose them is call you crazy, unhinged, and unstable. She never asked how Vinni was doing or why we believe these accusations are true. As an abuser, Ofelia only knows to attack and recruit flying monkeys for her circus.

Murder Dreams

My type of murder dream was like a daydream. I fantasized about what I wanted to happen, but unfortunately, it was murdering another human and not about being at the beach, or whatever normal people daydream about. Picture this. It's December 2021, and Carmen has just learned about Sergio molesting her grandsons and granddaughter. She has to play it cool and interact with Ofelia and the gang, so they don't suspect anything is up. The police have not yet brought Sergio in for questioning, so as far as the Delgados are concerned, everything must be normal. The biggest fantasy element in my murder dream was that Carmen would be a willing participant.

"What if Nana called Sergio up and was like, 'I made you some rice, do you want to come downstairs and eat?' Then she would feed him rice laced with poison. It needs to be tasteless. And colorless so he doesn't notice it in the food and eats the whole plate. But easy enough for your mom to mix in. And we will have to figure out the serving size, et cetera, to make sure it's potent enough. Once he croaks, she calls me and says, 'El cabrón está muerto,' and I immediately start driving to her house. Then we call Poncho and Denis so they can drag the body out and load it into my trunk. I'll drive down to Worcester Police Department and be like 'I fucked up. I murdered him. I'm wicked sorry. Where should I leave the body?' If Kyle Rittenhouse can cross state lines with an assault rifle, murder a random pedophile, AND get away with it, why can't I murder the one that is actually terrorizing my family? Isn't that actual self-defense?" I shared my murder dream with Felipe after he came home from work.

"Ricin. That's the poison we need." That was his response. He knew exactly which poison would be perfect for the job. He had learned about it on *Breaking Bad*. He really is a great husband and father. He complements me in many ways.

The first week after "entering the upside down," which is what it feels like when something like this happens, was full of adrenaline highs, but then ran out completely. My son told me about the sexual abuse on Monday. Tuesday, I called the pediatrician and spoke to DCF. Wednesday, I filed the police report and spoke with the District Attorney's office. Thursday, I called Carmen to check in and see how she was handling things. Friday, I picked up fancy macaron cookies to deliver to my favorite local clients. After a busy week of recounting the facts and details of Vinni's abuse to multiple authority agencies, it was Saturday, the end of the week. My plan for the day seemed easy compared to the week itself. I just had to deliver Christmas macarons to my clients and go to a dentist appointment.

That Saturday morning, I dropped the kids off with my parents. Felipe was working overtime. When I got home, I started sobbing. Mentally, I just couldn't go to the dentist. The thought of them criticizing my flossing or telling me I had a cavity, or bringing up receding gum line surgery—it all made me feel so fucking anxious. I cried and cried alone in my home, then called the dentist. I was sort of honest. I had just been to that office twice that week for my kids' appointments. When the lady answered, I asked, "Is this the lady with the multicolored hair or the other girl?" She said she was the other girl. I said, "OK, hi. I'm really sorry to do this, but I am experiencing a family emergency, and I cannot come to the dentist today. Mentally, I cannot come in, and I'm so sorry." I was crying by the time I finished what I had to say. The woman on the phone was really nice and understanding. She said someone would contact me later on about rescheduling my appointment.

Next, I tried to deliver some Christmas macarons to my clients. I made it to one salon that weekend and a second salon early the following week, but I could not bring myself to deliver all six dozen cookies. It was too hard. Pretending to be cheerful was not something I could do on command anymore. Sometimes fighting back the tears was all I could do. Sometimes I couldn't even do that. I definitely couldn't stop the murder dreams. And

I definitely ate four dozen macarons that week that I couldn't deliver to my clients.

It was shortly after this dentist/macaron fiasco that I called my doctor's office and asked to speak to the nurse. I told them I was having a really hard time dealing with my life and asked for a therapy referral. I started crying on the line, and they transferred me over to crisis management. The woman I spoke with at crisis management was really kind. She just let me unload some of my trauma onto her while she listened. Then she spoke about setting up my first therapy appointment. It's hard to get therapy nowadays. Everyone has a waitlist, and the available appointments she was seeing were weeks out. She suggested a group therapy session that I could join immediately, but I couldn't do that.

"Listen, I don't think I can do a group therapy thing. I have never done therapy in my whole life, and this is some really fucked up shit I'm dealing with right now. I just don't feel like I want to open my trauma up to a group of strangers right now. That feels so scary. I would prefer one-on-one therapy if that's possible." She said she would keep looking for a therapist that could see me as soon as possible and said she would call me back.

A little while later she did call. She said she had two questions for me. "Has DCF been notified about your son's sexual abuse?" I said, yes, we have notified the pediatrician, DCF, and the police. Then she asked, "Do you have any violent feelings of wanting to cause harm to the perpetrator who abused your son?"

I paused for several seconds. Does anybody, in my position actually respond with "no" to that question? I just said, "I'm not stupid enough to do anything stupid." I may not have shared my ricin murder dream with this lady, but I think she could sense my heightened emotions. She set me up with my therapist, Melanie, that same week. I've been meeting with her every two weeks since then to help me process my life.

Like I said earlier, this experience has been markedly different for me and for Trinny. I was having murder dreams in week one. Trinny wasn't ready to let go as easily. She's known Sergio since he was born. Grieving him as a nephew was much harder than it was for me. As soon as I found out how gross Sergio really is, it really made me think about how I didn't really know him as a person. He always gave me a hug when I saw him and would say very sweetly, "Hi Titi! I love you!" but I never had any real conversations with him. I would wish him a happy birthday but never texted with him. I wonder if this was intentional on his part, to avoid me, as his victim's mother. I never felt close to his father, Tony, either. Tony only spoke Spanish, though, so there was that language barrier on top of him being a pervert. The last time I hugged Tony was at Gloria's last gender reveal party. I felt him squash my chest into his, like he was trying to make his boobs feel up my boobs. Gross.

It may have taken a few months for Trinny to get to the murder dream level, but she did get there. Her murder dream was more of a nighttime dream though. She called me one day and said, "Erin, I am at my wit's end with these fucking evil-ass people. And I had a dream about Sergio last night. In my dream he rang the doorbell, and when I answered the door and saw it was him, and saw that stupid ass smile on his face, I completely lost it. I just immediately started strangling him. It felt so good to murder him in my dream."

I have never understood murder motives as clearly as I do now. With child molestation cases, it's unusual for the suspect to be caught in the act and arrested. We reported Sergio's crimes in December of 2021. As of July 1, 2022, he has not been arrested. At his arraignment, he was released on personal recognizance and told not to have any unsupervised visits with children under the age of sixteen. He didn't have to post bail. He doesn't have to wear an ankle bracelet. His arraignment was never in the newspaper. When you realize the scope of trauma that sexual abuse victims face, and experience the symptoms on a daily basis, your rage builds. The perpetrator is free to live his life while awaiting trial, only supervised by the same people that enabled the abuse for over a decade. So, you dream a little dream of murder.

Doña Ofelia

Today I asked my husband what his mom, Carmen, called her mother-in-law. He said "Doña Ofelia." I wonder if she demanded this title or if Carmen called her this on her own, as that is a common way of addressing an elder in the Latin culture. Adding "Don" or "Doña" before someone's name is used as an honorific title. It's a way of showing respect. In the mafia, the don is the leader of a crime family.

I don't have many memories of Doña Ofelia. I visited with her here and there while Felipe and I were dating. She came to my bridal shower and wedding. I remember she complained about my bridal shower starting so early. I explained to her, "It's a brunch. That's why it starts at 10:00 a.m. We're serving breakfast food." She didn't understand why the invitation was addressed to just her, either. Why wasn't her son, Felipe Sr., invited?

In my family, bridal showers and baby showers are frilly little parties where women gather together, exchange gifts from a registry list, and play cheesy games like Bridal Bingo. In Felipe's family, a party is an all-out party—never a boring little gift exchange. It didn't matter if it was a baby shower, bridal shower, a one-year-old's birthday party—it started at 6:00 p.m. and went all night long with beers, a DJ, etc. Everyone is invited too. Doña Ofelia wasn't the only one of my in-laws who thought my bridal shower was weird. It was one of many cultural differences we would learn about each other as Felipe and I merged our lives together.

Doña Ofelia came to see Olivia in the hospital when she was born. I also remember visiting with her while I was still pregnant. Doña Ofelia was telling me, "You must make sure you eat nice and healthy for the baby. Not too much junk food." As she lectured me, she was smoking a cigarette, and the smoke was making me nauseous. After that visit I talked to Felipe about my expectations after the baby was born.

Felipe Sr. and Doña Ofelia smoked cigarettes in their home. I never liked being in a smoky house, but I grew up around smokers, so it wasn't foreign to me. I told him if we bring the baby to their house after she's born, I don't want them to smoke around her. "Like I know it's their home and they can do what they want, but I don't want my newborn breathing in cigarette smoke." Felipe agreed.

Olivia was born in November. We went to Felipe Sr. and Doña Ofelia's house for Christmas Eve that year. She was only about two months old. Doña Ofelia agreed to smoke outside while we were visiting. Every time she went out for a smoke, she let everyone know how annoyed she was about this "no smoking around babies" thing. She layered up her clothing and mumbled about how freezing it was outside.

I think that was one of the last times I went to Felipe Sr. and Doña Ofelia's house. Over the next decade, I would see them sometimes, from a distance. They lived next door to Carmen's house. When Felipe Sr. and Carmen were married, they acquired two three-decker properties side by side. When they divorced, Carmen moved into 32 Arthur Street, and Felipe Sr. remained at the one next door, with his mother. Nineteen-year-old Junior moved in with Carmen. Doña Ofelia and Felipe Sr. were upset about Junior going to live next door.

Felipe always felt closer to his mother than to his father. He also felt a resentment toward Senior for the way his mom was treated. Carmen was hurt by Felipe Sr.'s constant infidelity. At the end of the day, she still loved him and didn't want the divorce. Junior went to stay with his mother, so she wasn't alone. His sisters both had families of their own. Felipe Sr., to this day, refers to Doña Ofelia as "Mami," and here he was criticizing his nineteen-year-old son for choosing to support his broken mother over his selfish-ass father.

Carmen was sixteen years old when she got married and Felipe Sr. was nineteen. They lived in Chicago with Doña Ofelia. They had four children, and when their youngest, Felipe Jr., was around three years old, they moved to Worcester, Massachusetts. Felipe Sr. was the boss of his household, but his biggest influencer and second in command was Doña Ofelia, not his wife, Carmen. It was common for Doña Ofelia to ride in the front seat of the car while Carmen rode in the back with the kids. It was normal for Carmen to stay home with their handicapped child, Zandra, while the rest of the family, Doña Ofelia, Felipe Sr., and the kids, went to church, shopping, or on vacation. In fact, people often assumed Felipe Sr. was married to Doña Ofelia until they were told Carmen was his actual wife.

Doña Ofelia was not a kind mother-in-law to Carmen. She competed with her in strange ways. If Carmen prepared food for the family, Doña Ofelia would make a second meal and try to get people to eat her food instead. She enticed Felipe Jr. away from his mother's dinner frequently. Doña Ofelia also complained about Carmen's cooking—things weren't cooked properly, had too much or too little salt, etc. Sometimes Doña Ofelia would give food to Carmen, saying, "Here, have some. Don't worry, I didn't make it spicy." Carmen would take one bite and be like that bitch did it again with the flaming hot food! She would look over at Doña Ofelia and Felipe Sr. sweating profusely as they ate the food she claimed wasn't too spicy. After Felipe Sr. and Carmen got divorced, Doña Ofelia would ask Carmen to make rice for her, so I guess she didn't hate Carmen's food after all.

Doña Ofelia used to cover up for her son's affair with his girlfriend, Charlene. Charlene was a married woman he worked with at the envelop company. Whenever Charlene gave Felipe Sr. a gift, Doña Ofelia would cover it up through her friend's son, Bolivar. Bolivar was a young man who supposedly received gift after gift that he could not keep, and he always gave them to his mother's friend, Doña Ofelia, to regift to her son.

Where'd Felipe Sr. get that new ring? "Oh, someone gave it to Bolivar, but he doesn't like gold." Where did Felipe Sr. get those new boots? "Oh, Bolivar bought them and brought them to a shoemaker, but they didn't fit him right afterward." Where did Felipe Sr. get that new shirt? "Oh, Bolivar received it as a gift, but it didn't fit him." Luckily for Felipe Sr., every time someone bought Bolivar a gift, it was the wrong size, wrong color, etc., but suited Felipe Sr. perfectly.

Doña Ofelia always lived with Felipe Sr. and Carmen. It was common for friends and family members to stay with them from time to time, like Maria and Felipe's uncle, Tío Lupe. At one point Carmen's mother, Cruzita, came to stay with them. Cruzita suffered from some mental health issues, but Felipe remembers her as a sweet, loving grandmother. He always preferred this grandmother to Doña Ofelia. One night, in the middle of the night, Felipe Sr. decided that Cruzita could not live there any longer. Carmen had to quickly pack up her bags and find shelter for her. Felipe doesn't know why his dad chose to throw Cruzita out on the streets that night, but he knows Doña Ofelia had something to do with it.

Ofelia Delgado certainly lives up to her namesake, Doña Ofelia. Ofelia is seven years older than Felipe. She was a nurturing older sister to him at times, but he remembers her also being cruel. When she was a teenager, she handed little eight-year-old Felipe a toy catalog that had come in the mail. She told him to circle all the toys he wanted, and she would buy them for him. Felipe was stoked. He circled matchbox cars, GI Joe action figures—whatever else was hot for toys back in the '90s. When he gave the catalog back to her, she laughed in his face and never bought him anything. At eight years old, he literally thought to himself, what the fuck was that? My sister Ofelia is a cunt.

Ofelia Delgado watched her grandmother Doña Ofelia lie, gaslight, and bully her mother, Carmen, her whole childhood. In terms of being the heir to a crime family, she's learned from the best, Doña Ofelia.

Therapy Kittens

My cousin Kelley works at a veterinary office. She is the closest thing I had to a sister growing up. She's four years older than me, and I spent most summers during my childhood sleeping over at her house. We went swimming, ate Bagel Bites and chicken nuggets, and played Bubble Bobble on Nintendo every single day. We also played Bargain Hunter, the best board game ever. We would fight and disagree sometimes, but I don't ever remember her being mean to me, as my big cousin. My relationship with her reminds me of my kids' relationship with their big cousin, Illianna.

I texted Kelley a couple months ago asking if she had any extra kittens lying around the vet office she works at. She told me she worked with a girl named Meghann who ran a cat rescue out of her home. Meghann had a litter of three kittens that would be ready for adoption soon. I didn't say anything to Felipe or the kids right away. Last October someone was looking to rehome a beautiful Ragdoll cat named Daryl. Olivia saw my text, and so she knew about the cat right away. The owner ended up changing his mind and decided to keep Daryl, so it was pretty devastating to think we were getting him and then we didn't. I wasn't saying shit until I knew these kittens were for sure going to be ours.

Kelley connected me with Meghann. There were two boys and one girl. She adopts kittens in pairs, so they have a friend to play with. This would be a good fit for our older cat too. The kittens would entertain themselves and hopefully leave Jazzy alone. They were not yet spoken for, so she asked if we wanted to come meet them and see which two kittens we would like to adopt. I finally told Felipe. His initial reaction, "What the fuck, Erin? Trevor just moved out. We can finally sleep at night without him yelling at the X-box, and now you want to get two kittens?"

"We could name them Joey and Chandler!"

"But then we would need a third to be Ross." Yes. He was getting sucked in already.

"Exactly, babe. I'm gonna order us three kittens." He laughed and said we really only needed two kittens, but OK, let's go meet them. I set up a time for us to go that Saturday. When Felipe got home from work the next day, we told the kids the news. I said, "Hey kids, on Saturday we need to go to this place in Douglas. They have some kittens and want us to see which two should come live with our family." All three of their jaws hit the floor.

"What??? We are getting kittens? Oh my God!!!! Two of them??? Oh my God!!!" The kids screamed with happiness. The hard moments had been plenty over the last six months, but this moment of pure excitement was bliss. They had one more day of school to get through that week, and then it was time to go meet our kittens.

I knew in my heart we were taking all three kittens before we even got to Meghann's house. Adopting two of them would really be us deciding which one not to take home, and as animal lovers, we were all completely incapable of doing that. As expected, as soon as we met them, I looked at Felipe and said, "But really, what is the difference between two or three kittens?"

He was trying to be strong and pointed out two perfect kittens we should adopt, but each of our kids fell in love with a different kitten. Even big, strong Felipe was the first to announce, "We need the orange one because it likes me." It had come right up to him when we walked in the room.

Olivia loved the little orange guy too. There was a black one with white double paws that looked like mittens. Vinni fell in love with this little guy. I did too! He came right up to me and climbed into my lap. The girl kitten was very playful and feisty. She would be a good hunter for the mice in our house, so we all agreed she needed to come with us.

Meghann was very sweet. She was like, "I understand you were planning to take two kittens, so just let me know once you guys talk it over." I really liked Meghann. She's younger than me, has a house full of cats, and she's working day after day to spay and neuter the stray cats she traps and releases. She truly loves cats and is dedicated to helping them.

It would be a couple weeks before we took them home. They had to get spayed/neutered and get some shots first. I felt a lot of anger during this waiting time. Anger toward Sergio and Ofelia. And anger toward Carmen for not choosing us as her family instead of them. Murder dreams were in full force. I finally broke down and started writing. Sometimes I write when I'm stressed. I've written two books at other times in my life.

I started writing this book, *Rotten Fruit Is Falling Down*. I also started drawing a lot with Luna. Flowers and butterflies are the subject matter. Lots of orchids—my favorite flowers. My own little version of art therapy to do with my kids. Another thing to pass the time while we waited for our kittens. Another coping mechanism to keep the murder dreams at bay.

We immediately started setting up Kittenland. The dining room would be where the kittens were isolated as they got acclimated to our home. We read that you should introduce new kittens to your older cat gradually. The kittens were used to living in Meghann's small room, so their new home was going to be their first big adventure. We set up a cat tower, multiple beds, two litter boxes, and a food zone. The dining room doesn't have doors on it, so we had to figure out how to seal it off while being able to go see them easily. Baby gates and a clear shower curtain did the trick.

Felipe never owned kittens before. So when Rosie cannonballed the water bowl twice within two hours of being home, he was like, "These things are fucking crazy!" They really are. Kittens are nuts. They are so cute and fluffy and soft though! And they run right up to you and they purr and they are everything we needed at that moment. Salem, Nacho, and Rosie were here now, our therapy kittens, to help us cope with life.

The System

I grew up visiting the Worcester Police Department (WPD) more often than the average child because my mother, Noreen, worked there. She answered the nonemergency phone line and worked in the communications department. She would wave and say hi to various officers as we navigated the cement building. Noreen was not the city of Worcester's best employee. She was mostly dedicated to office shenanigans, like coordinating Fear Factor Jell-O shots. She mixed random ingredients with flavorless gelatin, and weird people she worked with ate them. One guy said her blue cheese Jell-O shots were delicious.

Just a few years ago, I went to WPD routinely for budget meetings. I took a tour of the whole building once because I took my job seriously. If you were requesting a $500,000 roofing project, show me where it's leaking. They totally needed a new roof. It wasn't budgeted for the last year I worked at that job, but I hope it's been repaired by now.

December 2021 was my first time going to WPD as a victim of a crime. Each time I went there, I recognized an officer I knew. It was the one time I wished I didn't know so many people. Before I went to give my statement to the detective, I went to a wake. It was in December, before Christmas. My friend Jess had just lost her dad. Reilly said she would pick me up and we'd go to the wake together. I had completely forgotten about it until the day of, when Reilly reminded me.

I decided to wear my black snakeskin leggings and yellow Michael Kors T-shirt. I would be a little bit of sunshine on top, and Jess would appreciate me wearing hot pants to her dad's wake. I also brought her some cookies because wakes are long, and of all people, I knew Jess would be hungry. When we got to the funeral home, I noticed several people in uniform. I asked Reilly where Jess's dad worked. "He was the chief trial court officer at Worcester District Court. I'm sure there will be a million court officers here tonight."

I didn't know much about Jess's dad. There was a long line of people at the wake. We were all wearing masks because of COVID-19. We navigated the maze inside the funeral home. The line was stopped while we were about ten people away from the casket. Everybody stopped moving. A procession of trial court officers walked past us, down the line, by the casket and offered condolences to Jess and her family. It felt like it took about ten minutes for all of them to complete the procession. I recognized a guy I went to high school with. I looked at each passing officer's face and wondered who might be at court when I was there for Sergio's trial.

The day Trinny and I filed our police reports, I met her there. My office is next door to WPD on Union Street, so I just walked up to meet her. That morning I brought the kids to school and then brought Luna to my parents' house. They had just come home from a vacation and hadn't yet been told what Sergio did. I had a call scheduled with a client that morning, so I dropped Luna off and went to work without telling them the news. After my phone call was done, I called my mom. I told her what Vinni had told us while she was on vacation. She started crying. She was very angry, very sad, very heartbroken. I told her I was going to file the police report with Trinny, then was going home. She offered to keep Luna overnight, so I only had to worry about getting the kids at the bus stop.

When Trinny and I walked into the police station, we were both wearing masks. The officers behind the window were not, nor was the officer taking down our report. It was whatever officer was assigned to the area of 32 Arthur Street that day that would be the one taking our initial report. We waited in the lobby for a few minutes, and then he pulled up in his cruiser and came inside. We told him about Sergio right there in that lobby. The officer was young—I'd guess twenty-three to twenty-five years old. I recounted exactly what Vinni had told me.

The officer wasn't sure how to classify our reports at first. He'd never had a sexual abuse case involving first cousins before.

Because the predator also resided at 32 Arthur Street during some of the assaults, he wasn't sure if this should be considered domestic or not. He radioed his team or whoever was on the other end, to confirm how to label our case. Next, he took Trinny's story about what Illianna had told her.

The officer wrote down some notes and confirmed the main details with us. He also introduced us to the officer in charge of investigating sex crimes. That guy reassured us that they would all be communicating with the DA about our police reports and that we'd hear from the detective that gets assigned to us soon.

We report the crime to the police. They investigate the crime, gather evidence, and interview the players. The police and DA decide if and how to move forward with the case against the perpetrator. They are the gatekeepers. When the detective called to tell me about his interview with Sergio, he said, "You guys have a long road ahead if you want to move forward. Your son will have to testify in court if you choose to press charges, which might be difficult for him. I believe Vinni. And we have cause to charge Sergio with two counts of indecent assault and battery on a minor under fourteen years. Do you want to move forward with pressing charges?"

"Yes." Of course I wanted to press charges. I wanted Sergio in jail as soon as possible. Several people throughout this process, across multiple agencies, have asked me how I wanted to proceed. Apparently, it is common for people not to move forward with prosecuting family members for sexual abuse.

Some people have even specifically began sentences when talking to me with, "This is common in Hispanic families." That was another line that infuriated me. Don't talk to me about what typical Hispanic families are like. I have been part of the exact family in question for fifteen years, and we are not fucking typical, because of me, Erin Arvizu. And because of my son, Vinicio Arvizu.

Our next court date is July 19, about two weeks away. We'll be on vacation that week in New Hampshire, but Felipe and I are driving home for it. We aren't required to be there, just Sergio is, but I have to be there because of me. I have to see, with my own eyes, which circus clowns are there by his side. I need to hear when the trial date is set, as it's read aloud in court. I need the brief opportunity to speak with the prosecuting attorney and victim-witness advocate.

When Felipe and I go to court, we go down to the first level where the DA's office is. There, we wait to meet with the prosecuting attorney and our victim-witness advocate. Together, we walk upstairs to the assigned courtroom. It's much more VIP than the defense. Sergio and the circus just wait in the general waiting area before going into the courtroom. Almost every time I'm there, someone assumes I work there and asks me a question. I'm fast to brush them off and tell them I have no idea. I'm too busy feeling anxious about our case.

The DA office has said not to put certain things in writing because they could have to turn it over to the defense, and they will try and use it against us. This is hard for me. I want confirmation you heard the facts I gave you. I want a record that it was disclosed. I don't want the DA to forget what I said. It is for justice and for my own sanity that I put certain things in writing, so I have been doing that during this process.

I'm the mother of the victim and a key witness in this case. I have never navigated this system before, but every single person I speak to works with cases like mine every single day. Some are desensitized and insensitive. I can't wait to be on the other side of the system, with this trial behind us.

Last month, a defense attorney from Worcester requested to connect with me on LinkedIn. I'm not sure how he found me or why he would want to connect with me. Maybe he just assumes all accountants want to be connected to attorneys. I went to his website and saw that defending sexual abuse charges was an area of expertise for him, so I deleted his request. I refuse to be connected to any part of the system that defends sex offenders.

Deadly Blessing

Facebook memories are a trip when you live a life like mine. Yesterday was the Fourth of July. A July Fourth memory from 2020 popped up on my Facebook. It had a picture of a red, white, and blue cake I made with the kids, also pictures of my kids. They were wearing bathing suits in this picture because they had been playing on the water slide in our backyard and Vinni did not have a shirt on. On the surface, it looks like a normal social media memory of happy kids and patriotic food. Then I saw the first comment from July 4, 2020. It read, "Happy fourth! I love you and miss you all so much!" The comment was from Sergio Delgado.

That Fourth of July was about four months into the COVID-19 pandemic. My kids stopped going to school on March 13, the day after Felipe's birthday. We didn't know at the time we would all be trapped at home, homeschooling our kids, for what felt like an eternity, but that's what happened. By July 4, 2020, Sergio had not had access to Vinni for four months.

My good friend Kerri was an intensive care nurse during a big chunk of the COVID-19 pandemic, including those very early days. She was one of those frontline nurses wearing ten-day-old N95 masks with red marks and lines dug into her face. She cared for person after person as they died alone, with their families on the other end of a smartphone. She slept on the couch in the basement of her home because her husband has asthma, and she was deathly afraid of bringing this virus home to her family. She lost her mom that year. 2020 was a deadly year for her and so many others.

I had just launched my new accounting business that January. I quit city hall that fall. My new business specializes in providing accounting services to salons, but by March 2020, COVID-19 had caused a massive shutdown. No school, no restaurants, no salons. Just grocery stores and essentials. Even construction at Polar Park, where the Woo Sox play, was shut down at one point.

I had no choice but to freeze my business, homeschool my kids, and cook every single day. I baked pies from scratch. I grew a big, beautiful garden. I saw an oriole in my backyard for the first time. I wrote a book—a book that is much different than this one. It was an accounting organizer book for salon entrepreneurs that teaches them how to do their own bookkeeping. We watched *Moana* and *Frozen 2* on Disney+ every single day. The kids and I never left the house. Felipe went to work, and I had groceries delivered. Mentally, I felt like I was losing my mind, but my kids were home, and they were safe.

They didn't go to Nana's house or my parents' house because everyone was quarantining. Little by little things started opening back up, and vaccines were distributed. If you got COVID-19 in 2020, like my aunt Patty, it was scary. If you got COVID-19 at the end of 2021 like I did, it was more of a nuisance.

Sergio got COVID-19 pretty early on. He became sick and tested positive. Ofelia couldn't even tell the truth about his diagnosis. She told Carmen, "No, Mami, his test showed traces of COVID particles, but he wasn't positive." I think she was probably justifying why Sergio didn't quarantine.

My family and I dodged COVID-19 for quite a while. We made it all 2020 and most of 2021 before I fell as its first victim. I went to my twenty-year high school reunion the Friday after Thanksgiving in 2021. By Tuesday night of the following week, I didn't have much of an appetite at dinner and went to bed early. By Wednesday afternoon I felt like absolute shit and had a fever.

My parents were babysitting Luna that day. I went to work for a few hours, then went home. It was around 2:35 p.m. I had to walk up to the bus stop to get the kids in ten minutes. I had an at-home COVID-19 test kit, so I swabbed my nose, left it on the counter, and walked up to get the kids. I wore a face mask. Before I even left the house, I saw the COVID-19 test already had two lines. I've taken pregnancy tests like that before. Instantly, I was positive.

The kids were surprised to see me wearing a mask. I told them I didn't feel good and was worried I had COVID-19. When we got home, Olivia saw the positive test and immediately started sobbing. "I can't believe you got COVID, Mom! What if you get really sick?!" She was so scared. COVID-19 was a deadly virus for some people and now I had it.

I reassured her I was going to be fine. I had already made myself some chicken soup and after a few days of rest, I would be feeling better. Vinni cried when he heard about the COVID-19 result too. I was the first person in my kids' inner circle to contract the virus, and I was the center of their whole world.

When Felipe came home from work, we came up with our family's COVID-quarantine plan. I would sleep in Luna's bed and use only the blue bathroom, while the family used the other non-COVID bathrooms. I would wear a mask whenever I had to venture outside my bedroom. Felipe was also overly annoying with the Lysol spray. I swear he sprayed that damn spray every time I moved an inch or touched anything. I wasn't bothered by the smell, however. "Wow, that has zero scent to it. I figured it would be really strong smelling."

He just looked at me with his T-shirt up over his nose, while he continued to spray and said, "It smells very strong. You lost your sense of smell." I guess I had. That was one of the telltale signs you had COVID-19.

My kids had a very hard time with me quarantining away from the family. They would stand in my doorway and cry. They had no idea, and neither did I, that not hugging your mom for more than a day was absolute torture! We eventually loosened up on the rules, and we had a blanket that I would wrap them up with and hug them. This was so they could feel me hug them, but still had a barrier from my COVID-19 cooties. The blanket hugs became a routine. I remember the three of them lined up waiting for their blanket hug before bedtime and there was Felipe at the end of the line waiting for one too.

I think we quarantined for ten days. That first Saturday I could hug my kids freely and leave the house was a big celebration for us. Me and all three kids went to get our nails done at the salon in Tatnuck Square. Luna requested waffles with whipped cream for breakfast. Apparently, that's what Olivia had been making her every morning while I was in quarantine. Things were a bit off the rails, but my kids helped each other and grew more independent during that time.

That Monday, December 13, 2021, would be their first day back at school and Luna's first day going to Nana's again. I remember Vinni asking me that morning if Grampa was picking them up at the bus, and I said, "No. I'm picking you and Livi up, and then we're getting Luni at Nana's. So you guys aren't staying at Nana's today." He was relieved. I asked him all the time why he hated going to Nana's because it was something he said every week. He never gave me a clear answer until that night.

That Monday was the night Vinni shared his truth with me. Those first days afterward were very raw for me. Folding his laundry made me cry—his clothes are so small still. Thinking about how many times he went to Nana's house made me sob. Vinni seemed like he felt freer, though. His secret was released. He knew he would never go to that house again. If you ask him what the worst thing that happened to him was, he won't say Sergio. He'll say, "The time my mom got COVID." That means the world to me. Sergio did not break him and never will.

COVID-19 ended up being a deadly blessing for us. It was a deadly, scary virus, but shutting the world down protected Vinni for many months. It took him away from that god-awful routine with Sergio. I'm sure Sergio did miss Vinni that Fourth of July, but we never missed him—not for a single second, and we never will.

Tonito

In 2021, my family's Disney movie of choice was *Encanto*. Another movie we watched religiously, pretty much every morning and maybe even every afternoon. The songs are great. It's about a Latin family, the Madrigals. Our only beef was one character named Antonio, whom they refer to as Tonito, twice in the movie.

When I met Sergio, he was a child, and I met him as Tonito. His father's name is Anthony, or Tony, as we call him. Referring to Sergio as Tonito means "sweet little Tony." Adding "ito" to someone's name is a familial term of endearment. I called him Tonito for the first fourteen years that I knew him and considered him my nephew. I didn't even know his real name was Sergio Anthony Delgado until I got a friend request from him on Facebook. His family never calls him Sergio. When Vinni told us his truth, I knew immediately that "Tonito" was a fictitious person. It was just the version of Sergio he presented to his family.

I'm curious to know the version of Sergio he presents to Becca to keep her not only in love with him, but continuing to defend his innocence despite four victims already coming forward. Or does she not know there are four? We don't know what Sergio and Becca's relationship is like, but with Ofelia as her mother-in-law, we know her life isn't peaceful.

We stopped referring to him as Tonito immediately. He will now forever be known as a monster named Sergio.

Sergio works as a masonry worker and has for a while. He owned a business called Midas Masonry at one point, but I don't know where he works now. A long time ago, when Vinni was little, Sergio and his father, Tony, were rebuilding a set of cement stairs in front of someone's house. When they were finished, the work looked nice, but after a big rain, the bricks began sinking into the dirt, separating from the landing. They had not laid the proper foundation for the stairs. The people who hired this company were pissed! They paid a lot of money to have their stairs redone, and here they were, completely unsafe to walk on, and how the hell do they fix it? Tony said, "The company didn't tell us to lay that foundation, so we just built the stairs without it. It's not our fault, it's the company's."

I know this happened because I saw it with my own eyes. When Olivia was born, my mom told me her friend Mary ran an at-home day care not too far from my house. She said if her grandbabies went to day care, they had to go to the best, and that was Mary. I called Mary, and she was able to start watching Olivia one day a week when I went back to work after she was born.

Eventually all three kids went to Mary's house, and to this day, they still all say, "I miss going to Mary's!" I even wish sometimes I could just drive up and drop them all off at her house! We feel very lucky to have had such a loving caregiver for our kids. Mary's house was always super spotless. She is a very organized person and had the perfect day care area set up for the kids. We would pull into the driveway, ring the garage doorbell, and then walk up the basement stairs to the kitchen, where we dumped off our babies and their lunches. Don't even think about walking up to the kitchen with your shoes on though—there were multiple signs reminding you to remove your shoes. Shoes were forbidden past the basement. Even her basement was spotless. Mary would absolutely die if she saw the size of the spider colony that lives in my basement.

It was back when Olivia and Vinni were little, before Luna was born. I pulled up at Mary's to drop the kids off as usual, and there they were, working on her front steps, Sergio and Tony. I said hi to them and, "Such a small world you're working on my day care lady's front steps!" When the steps started separating from the landing, sinking into the ground, Mary and her husband were pissed. It was awkward for Felipe and me. We did not recommend this company to Mary, but she knew that we knew Sergio and Tony. She saw me talking to them while they were working that day.

Felipe asked Tony why he didn't lay the proper foundation for the steps. Felipe doesn't work in masonry, but as a tradesman, he knows a lot about stuff like this. That's when Tony told Felipe about it not being his fault, saying it was the company's fault. Tony had been working in masonry for years though. I couldn't understand why Tony would knowingly do a shitty job and not advocate for the required foundation even if the company overlooked it.

I remember apologizing to Mary and saying I couldn't stand the Delgado family, and this was just one more example of how they're pieces of shit. Another example of Tony's shitty-ass work brings us back to 32 Arthur Street. When Carmen moved into that apartment after her divorce, Tony offered to fix up the living room for her. He replaced all of the sheetrock and plastered, but he and Carmen never discussed pricing. When Carmen received a bill for over a thousand dollars, she was upset. She hadn't realized the project was going to be so expensive. Tony felt bad and offered to redo her kitchen floor for free—she only had to purchase the materials.

Carmen picked out ceramic tile and grout, and Tony installed her brand-new tile, right on top of the hardwood floor. The wood below started expanding due to moisture, and one by one, each tile started popping up. Carmen was furious! And so was Felipe. He told Tony not to just lay the tile on the wood before he even started the project. Felipe told him he had to lay a cement subfloor first. Tony didn't listen and cut corners on this project too. Felipe ended up ripping all that tile up and laid a new linoleum floor for his mom, which is still there today.

Felipe would sometimes bump into Tony and Sergio on the jobsite, at work. The last time this happened, Sergio was still Tonito to Felipe. It was a job in Boston, and all the trades were working simultaneously on different areas of the building. It was before December 13, 2021. For us, that's the day Tonito died and Sergio the monster was revealed.

The Blunt One

I was born and raised in Worcester, Massachusetts. I graduated from Framingham State College. I have one younger brother, Mikey, who also has that abortion to thank for being alive. My mom went from being told she wouldn't be able to have babies to having two babies eighteen months apart.

My parents both come from large families, and each have five siblings. After my brother was born, my mother got her one tube tied so she wouldn't get pregnant again. She said they originally wanted four kids, but after having us two—that was plenty. My mom started working at WPD when I was ten years old. Her shift was 3:00 p.m. to 11:00 p.m., so during the week it was just my dad and the kids after school and for dinner. My mom would call us during her supper break. Sometimes she would go to my Gramma and Papa's house for supper, and we would join her there.

My dad did a pretty good job cooking for us each night. Some meals were sinkers, like this "yummy pork chops" recipe he tried, but he always promised us fast food or pizza on Fridays, and we had to take turns with who got to choose dinner each week. One time my mom took a Friday off from work. When we came home from school, she was busy cooking a big pork roast dinner. Mikey and I were so fucking pissed! Fridays were take-out night. How dare she serve us home-cooked food!

My dad worked for the United States Postal Service from before I was born until just a couple years ago, when he retired. He always worked a lot of overtime during the holidays. He never had Saturday/Sunday off when I was younger. His days off were Sunday/Monday. It was tough getting a weekend bid with the hours he wanted, which was ass crack of dawn until early afternoon.

When he was turning forty years old, my mom planned a big surprise party for him on a Saturday. The plan was he would go to work that day, and my mom would set everything up for the party. Then when he got home from work, all the guests would be there, and it would be a great surprise party.

Right before the big day, my dad told my mom he was using a vacation day for that Saturday since it was his birthday. She called his boss at the post office and asked him to deny it. He was like what the fuck, Noreen, I don't want to do that, but I understand you're trying to plan this big party for him, so OK, fine. He denied my dad's vacation day. My dad was pissed. His boss had no real reason for denying his time off request. And it was his birthday!

So my dad submitted a personal day request and threatened to file a grievance with the union if it was denied. His boss was like, "Sorry Noreen, he's not working on Saturday." My mom was so mad at my dad for being home and ruining his surprise party. But then she made him set everything up in the backyard for her. It ended up being a fun party, as far as I remember, as one of the kids. It's weird. I'm about to turn forty soon, and my kids are around the age I was during that time.

My brother lives in Arizona with his wife and kids. I would call him a perfectionist. He always studied very hard and got good grades. He works as an engineer and is very successful at what he does. He has a master's degree and some other credentials that I don't really remember, but trust me, he's a wicked smart engineer. He is sometimes completely appalled by me.

I worked at city hall for about four years. For the second time in my life, I quit my job without having another one lined up. I knew it was the right decision to make and exactly how I was going to tell my boss. I asked my brother if he could proofread my resignation letter. He was once again lecturing his older, crazy-ass sister. "Erin. You can't write swear words in your resignation letter. You don't want to burn bridges, do you? It's not professional." I told him I was professional AF.

I met Felipe when I was twenty-three years old, and we started dating right before my twenty-fourth birthday. I fell in love with him instantly. The first time we kissed was at our friend Shayne's house. 32 Arthur Street is just around the corner from where he lives. My parents probably thought I was sleeping at my friend Reilly's. I actually slept at 32 Arthur Street that night and have never left his side since that day. That first morning we woke up together, Felipe asked me, "Do you want to meet my mom?"

I said, "No!" I did not want to meet his mom. I knew I was seeing him later that day, but I had no plans of meeting his family that morning. As he walked me out of his house, his mom was standing in the back hallway. I had no choice but to greet Carmen. Did she think of me as some slut?

Our meeting was brief. I shook her hand, Felipe introduced us. We both smiled and said, "Nice to meet you." After I left, she told him she loved my blue eyes and that she instantly had a vision that I would be her daughter-in-law. I thought she was crazy, but I didn't care. I loved her son already. My mom always told me I would know when I met the right guy I wanted to marry, and I felt that as soon as we started dating.

He never made me feel insecure or like he wasn't interested in being with me. He referred to me as his girlfriend right away. He was genuine. I was completely comfortable around him very soon. One of his favorite stories is our second date. Felipe owned four vehicles when I met him. He had a badass Cadillac CTSV that I would borrow sometimes and felt cool as hell cruising around with my girlfriends. He had an old beat-up Honda Civic that he used for commuting to work. The passenger door didn't open, so the first time I rode in it, I had to climb in through the back. It was better on gas mileage than the caddy. He had an old pickup truck. I don't even remember what the make/model was, but it was like a semi reliable, shitty old truck. He had this one because, "You never know when you might need a truck." He had a 1995 Mustang that he'd had since high school. That was his sentimental car that he fixed up himself.

Our second date was the day after I slept over at his house. We were going out to dinner. I had already met his mom once and shaken her hand, so it was expected that I hugged her every single time I saw her from then on. Sometimes I would forget and just do a wave and a "heeyyy" as I greeted Carmen. He'd nudge me and be like, "Go hug my mom." My family was affectionate, and we said "I love you" often, but I didn't immediately hug my mom first thing, every time I saw her. Another cultural difference we noticed right away.

He asked if I could drive that night because the caddy was due for an oil change. I said sure. As I was driving to pick him up, I don't know what happened. Maybe I forgot we were only on date number two because in my daydreams I was already marrying him on a beach in Hawaii, but right as I stopped in front of his house, I farted inside the car, with the windows rolled up. He opened the door with a big smile on his face to greet me, and a puff of fart air met him right back. He burst out laughing and was like, "Did you fart in here? What the fuck, Erin? I can't believe you farted in the car right before I got in!"

I became so instantly embarrassed, I'm sure I turned beet red. I denied everything. "No! I did not fart! That's trash juice or dog shit on the street or something. Just get in!"

He continued laughing all the way to TGI Fridays. "I can't believe you farted in the car on our second date." I told him to shut up. That smell was trash juice or dog shit on the street, not me! We went to dinner, and I slept over at his house again. Before I left my parents' house that night, I did not say I was sleeping at Reilly's. I said, "Bye, Mom, I'm having dinner with Felipe. I'll be home tomorrow." This was not what she wanted to hear, because I had just started dating him the day before, but it was the truth.

My oldest daughter is eleven years old now, about to start sixth grade in the fall. Her friends started being taller than me last year. I'm only four feet, eleven inches tall, so I am considered short, always the shortest among my friends and coworkers. I do have some height on some of my short-ass family members, though. I'm much taller than my cousin Kelley, who clocks in at only four feet ten.

When I'm wearing comfy clothes and no makeup, I look much younger and much more childlike than when I'm put together, dressed like a miniature adult. At twenty-seven years old, I was six months pregnant with Olivia. Felipe and I went to the movies, and the teenager that was working behind the ticket counter asked to see my ID because it was an R-rated movie. I flashed my wedding rings and pregnant belly and was like, "You think I might be younger than seventeen years old? Jeez Louise!" I showed my ID and continued on. Not too long before that, I got in for free at a craft fair because someone assumed I was under twelve.

Last June I got a big tattoo on my right forearm. "The world will know from here on out that I am not a child. I am an Earth Goddess." I unveiled my cool-ass tattoo to Felipe and the kids. They liked it. My Earth Goddess sits with her legs crossed, cradling the world in her arms. A lotus flower blooms beneath her from a stump, not water. The sun and moon are above her head. She is beautiful! A guy named Dan was the tattoo artist. He is amazingly talented and someone I've known since elementary school.

Ofelia told Olivia she didn't like my tattoo because the Earth Goddess sits facing me, not others. When Olivia shared this with me, I said, "Good thing I don't give a flying fluffernutter what Ofelia thinks, right?" My bluntness also rubbed off on my kids. One time Vinni was at City Hall with me. He was young, maybe four-ish years old. I was showing off my adorable son to all of my coworkers and then stopped by my boss's office.

He liked my kids, and my kids liked saying hi to him when they were there. Vinni went right up to the CFO at city hall and said, "Do you want to know why my mom doesn't like you?" My jaw hit the floor and I feared for my life as I waited for him to say what he was going to say. I talked a lot of shit about this dude at home, so God knows what kind of truth will emerge from my Vinicio. He giggled and said, "You make her go to too many budget meetings!" We all laughed, and I let out a big sigh of relief. That was a true statement and far from the worst thing he could have said.

He was the last boss I had, the CFO at city hall. He once told me the reason why the city manager didn't like me was because I was too blunt. It's funny how the word "blunt" means both not sharp and straight to the point. I remember specifically being blunt to the city manager in a budget meeting.

The police department had requested a new roof for $500,000 and two new generators, which were around one million, if I remember correctly. That year I visited a bunch of city-owned buildings as I made my way through departmental budget meetings. The city had hired an outside consultant to do a feasibility study on our buildings that year too—to come up with the best plan of maintaining them all, and to analyze which buildings/projects should be prioritized. My work coincided with the consultants' goals, and I worked closely with them as I compiled the city's capital budget requests.

The city manager loved funding park projects, and this irritated me as a taxpayer, especially as someone who worked so closely to our funding decisions. I agree with wanting our parks to be maintained and clean. I would prefer more effort being put into that, instead of elaborate, million-dollar turf fields. I also think our city needs more public bathrooms for the homeless population. Maybe fewer people would piss and shit in the Federal garage elevator if there was a public bathroom available.

Mr. Manager, which is what I was expected to call him, said he thought the police department would be happy with their capital budget fulfillments. He was sitting at the head of the conference table where he always sat, and I was seated to his right. I responded to his comment bluntly. I said, "I think the police will be upset you chose not to fund their roof and generators." The roof was leaking. I took pictures of water spots and noted several examples. One of the generators had failed earlier that year, and it had to be repaired. The diesel spill cleanup that resulted was not cheap.

Mr. Manager looked at me and said, "How dare you say that? I'm funding the repair for their crumbling cement stairs in the back parking lot. I funded their other cement stairs in the front in this fiscal year! And I'm funding the cruisers they requested! And tactical gear! That really ticks me off that you just said that." I didn't say another single word at that meeting.

He treated me like a stupid asshole. We spent hundreds of thousands of dollars on that consultant study that concurred with a lot of my recommended budget requests. In that feasibility study, they concluded the police department needed those repairs, as an older building in the city.

I also wrote in my budget notes that year that the library was one of our best buildings because it was much newer, built in the 2000s. The feasibility study rated this building in good shape too. Guess what Mr. Manager funded that year though? A nine million dollar project to shift the library's front door from the side of the building to the back. How dare I gripe about not funding the police station roof and generator? I did notice how nice the back staircase turned out when I walked up it at WPD to report Sergio's crime.

I think Felipe's family considers me to be blunt as well. I know Trevor does. When he came down the stairs at 11:01 a.m. and asked for a ride to work, I asked him, "What time does your shift start?" He said it started at eleven. I said, "You're already late. Doesn't that bother you?"

"Not really," he replied.

"Seriously? You just don't give a shit?"

"Not really."

"You're not worried about getting in trouble or getting fired?"

"No." I told him I for sure would fire his ass if he were one of my employees. He obviously didn't give a shit about his work ethic, and I would never tolerate that in an employee. As I drove him to work, I told him he had to give a shit about himself, give a shit about his job, give a shit about his girls. I love Trevor. How could I not tell him the truth about what I thought?

I think Trevor was learning I'm a different kind of "mean" than what he's used to. Ofelia and her children were mean, the way she was mean. They find pleasure in tormenting and dragging people down. I have no interest in doing that to the people I love. My meanness comes from blunt honesty. I'm going to be straight to the point, especially if I love you. I will hold you accountable.

Sometimes I just can't hold it in! I say things. I get in trouble sometimes. I've told my mother-in-law Carmen to "go fuck yourself" twice so far this year, and it's only July. I have said absolutely nothing to Ofelia, however.

During the interim time period, before Sergio was questioned by the police, Ofelia texted me. It was Christmas Eve, and she asked me what size shoe Vinni wore. I never responded. She would never give him a Christmas gift ever again, so it didn't matter what size she bought.

It wasn't the first time I left her on "read." Just a couple months before that, Ofelia texted me asking for the name and number of my friend who works for DCF. I didn't know what or who she wanted to report, but she could do so through the proper DCF channel, the way I did when I reported her granddaughter Mia possibly being molested by Sergio.

Ofelia knows I'm blunt. If she called me, I would demand to know why she thought her son was innocent. If she really did not believe what Vinni said was true, then why was the door always closed? What was Sergio's explanation? Why was Mia in there? Why did she make that comment that one time about wanting to rip Sergio's door off the hinges because she didn't trust him? Ofelia never confronted me because she knows I know the truth about Sergio, the truth about her, her husband, her whole ass family.

Bluntly speaking, I am 100 percent that bitch who will write an entire book about you and your crime family before your trial date is even set.

Last Call with Carmen

A few months into dating Felipe, I heard Carmen refer to me as "Mamita." I asked Felipe why she called me this. Did she think I was pregnant or something? He explained it was a sweet way to address me, like she thinks of me as her daughter. I thought Carmen was a very sweet woman, and I liked her right away.

I am hesitant to try new foods, and this is offensive to my husband's family. I'm sorry, everyone. I do not like tasting unknown food because I feel bad if I don't like it. I would rather stick to food I know. I've come a long way, believe it or not. After I graduated college, I started eating pasta with sauce on it and even tried lasagna. All this time I had refused to stray from spaghetti with butter, but adding sauce and cheese was actually delicious. Later in life, I also discovered that gravy on Thanksgiving is transformational. I never really enjoyed Thanksgiving dinner or got the hype until the one year I caved and added gravy. Holy shit, turkey was delicious!

I had come far from my childhood lunches of deconstructed sandwiches but still had strong food boundaries in my early to mid twenties. I would try certain foods now, but not everything, and I did have some regrets. Illianna was around four years old when she was slurping down pickled pig ears one day and offered me one. I politely declined and everyone was like, "Come on!! Try one!" Feeling the pressure, I caved and tasted a tiny piece. Nope, not for me—too oniony, the texture is weird. My kids love them though.

My favorite food that Carmen makes is her pork shoulder and rice and beans. The pork is slow cooked all day long, seasoned with oregano, garlic, salt, and pepper. Her rice has the perfect flavor and contains green olives, sausage, and pigeon peas. It may have taken twelve years of marriage, but Felipe says I mastered cooking the pork. He will tell you my rice needs work still.

Maybe it's because I'm Irish and have a genetic, built-in craving for potatoes, or maybe it's because my dad never really cooked rice and my mom only made pilaf, but I suck at rice. When we first moved in together, Felipe asked, "Hey, can you make white rice with dinner tonight?" I said sure. White rice was not my favorite, but I was fine with switching up the side dish for dinner that night.

I followed the instructions on the box and prepared plain white rice. Felipe took his first bite and was like, "What happened to the rice? It has absolutely no flavor." I just kinda looked at him like duh, that's why I stick to potatoes, white rice sucks.

He was like, "No, when my mom makes white rice, it tastes delicious. It has flavor." Well, as a white girl with food issues, I certainly did not know how to make delicious rice like his mom. The best I had in me was pilaf.

My kids love Nana's rice too—all different versions. Anytime I serve potatoes other than French fries, they protest. When Olivia was little, she would demand Nana's rice over my side dishes all the time. One time Vinni told me I was the best cooker ever, well, with one exception. "Except not your rice. Nana is the best rice cooker."

I've grilled my mother-in-law on how to make her rice. She explained the *sofrito* process. I looked up instructions online. My sister-in-law Trinny gave me some tips, like not stirring after it's no longer soupy. Each attempt I make tastes better than the last, but I have a long way to go before my rice stands a chance against Carmen's. It's not just her rice that we miss.

Carmen was a very loving Nana to my kids. The Spanish lullaby she sang to them was "A la ru-ru niño." Felipe also sings this to them. They would request it from me sometimes at bedtime, but I don't know it. Just like Felipe doesn't know "Hush Little Baby." I love how our family has both of our cultures smashed in, with everything we do.

I feel terrible about our last call with Carmen. It was a Sunday. The day before, Saturday, we were all at Trinny's house for Je'Nise's fifth birthday. Trinny had just moved into her house five days earlier and was already hosting a party. I knew Ofelia had already visited with Carmen at her new house, and I was upset about it. My whole family was. I wasn't sure if Carmen and Poncho would be at the party, but if they were, I was going to say something.

They didn't go to the party. Carmen texted Felipe the following day saying she loved him. He loves his mom too, but this type of interaction was wearing on him. He would tell her, over and over again, how he felt. His family was hurting because of what Sergio did. How could she possibly still speak to Ofelia, who was defending him tooth and nail? When he showed me her text the day after avoiding the party, I said, "Let's call her on speakerphone." I prefer to face things, even if it ends in explosion, rather than suppress and drag it out.

Vinni also wanted to talk to Nana if he saw her at the party. There is no neutral ground between the abuser and the victim. Neutrality only helps the oppressor, never the oppressed. We invited him to the speakerphone call. When Carmen answered, Felipe started out first. "Hi, Ma. I am here with Erin and Vinni on speakerphone. We want to talk to you together. I'm going to let Vinni go first."

Vinni moved closer to the phone and spoke very honestly. He said, "Nana, why do you choose Ofelia? Why don't you choose to be on our side?"

Carmen started responding, but in Spanish. This irritated me. She was choosing to only communicate with Felipe, knowing Vinni and I didn't understand what she was saying. I told Felipe, "No, no, no. Ask her to speak in English, so we all understand."

Felipe chimed in and said, "Ma, please. Why is it OK for Ofelia to come visit you, then go to court the next day and lie? They are fighting against us!"

She said loud and clearly, "Junior, you know I can't do this! Vinni needs to see a psychiatrist."

That remark really pissed me off. I said, "Yeah and so does Trevor and all of Sergio's victims! He caused so much pain to this family by abusing everyone. If you don't cut out those enabling pieces of shit, then you can go fuck yourself!"

"OK, Erin, that's nice. Thank you for that, Erin." Carmen's response was completely unexpected on my end.

Confused, yet fired up, I just said, "You're welcome, Carmen?"

"You all need therapy. Don't ever call this number again." We hung up with Carmen after she said that. We haven't spoken to her since. We miss her and want our Nana back. We don't know how to wake her up. We don't know how to fix this piece of our family.

Cutting out the Delgados did not hurt. We found relief in removing the toxicity from our life. Losing Carmen, due to our unbudgeable stance against abusers and enablers—this is complete heartbreak. It's a side of sexual abuse you don't really understand until it's happening inside your own family. You grieve people who are still alive.

Falling Down

I had a dream about Becca last night. It felt like we were good friends. We were hanging out at a bar, talking. I confronted her about Sergio. I asked why he isolated Vinni each week. And why was the door always closed? And why was Mia in the room? She did not respond much to these questions, but our conversation never elevated. She said she would still follow through with their wedding reception next year, as long as Sergio doesn't go to jail. Then we were walking, and we bumped into a friend of hers. She stopped to say hi and gave her a hug. The next thing I remember, Becca and I were watching a video, and in it, we saw Sergio kiss the friend that Becca had just seen. She looked surprised and hurt to see this video. I asked her, "Did you know he kisses other girls?" She didn't say anything in response. Then I woke up.

I don't remember my dreams often, but this one was very clear. It made me wonder about how Becca was doing and if she would be at court on Tuesday. Had she and Sergio discussed the contents of discovery in detail? By discovery, I'm referring to the police reports and whatever else the prosecution handed over to his defense attorney. Does Becca know he sexually abused Vinni for four years, the entire time they were dating? Does she remember his excuses for having to be at Ofelia's house on the days Vinni was at Nana's?

In my dream she seemed content with denying everything. She told me as long as Sergio is not convicted, she will marry him in front of all her family and friends at her big, fancy wedding reception. Did seeing footage of him cheating represent some kind of truth being unveiled? I had this dream about a week before our court date.

July 19, 2022, finally arrived, and we went to court. We drove home from our vacation rental in New Hampshire. We parked right on Main Street. As we were crossing the street to walk into the courthouse, we noticed Sergio and Becca were walking directly in front of us. They noticed too and veered down a side street to avoid being near us. It's obvious Sergio is embarrassed to face his victim's parents.

The usual circus clowns were in attendance to support Sergio—Becca, Ofelia, Estela, Felipe Sr., Maria, and Angel. Doña Ofelia also made her debut at court that day. Additionally, Becca's father and Becca's sister were there. Becca's sister is only seventeen years old. We went downstairs and met with our victim-witness advocate like we usually do. Then we walked into the courtroom together. We sat down on the left side of the court because the circus was seated to the right. The DA was responding to another matter but would be coming to speak to us in a little bit. Not too long after we all sat down in the courtroom, a recess was called, and we all exited into the lobby area. As Doña Ofelia walked by, she shook her head at us in disgust. In her mind, we are the enemy for prosecuting the family pedophile.

Recesses are usually kind of awkward for two reasons. Number one, it's awkward because we and the Delgado circus are all left waiting in the lobby area. We maintain distance and refrain from interacting with each other, but it's obvious we are both talking shit about the other side. The second cause of awkwardness is that you never know who you might see at court. While we were hanging around waiting for court to resume, we saw our neighbor from across the street walking by. She is an attorney, and her husband is a former Worcester city councilor. She locked eyes with Felipe, so he waved and smiled. She probably noticed we were waiting outside courtroom 15, which is for criminal cases.

When court resumed, we went inside and sat on the left side of the room again, while the Delgado clan sat on the right. Anytime I glanced over in their direction, I saw Ofelia staring me down with the ugliest face she could make. The DA came into the courtroom a few minutes later. She was wearing a purple dress. I saw her talking to Sergio's attorney. We were seated in the first row. She came over to speak to me. She greeted us kindly and then gave us an update.

"Hi, Erin, how are you all doing? Are these your parents?" She noticed my mom and dad had joined us at court that day. Illianna was also there as well as our friend Eric. I nodded my head yes. "Sergio's attorney is advising him to plead guilty to the charges. He needs more time to discuss this with him and convince him to change his plea, but I wanted to tell you that's the advice his attorney is giving him."

I almost burst into happy tears in that moment. Sergio's defense attorney does not want to go to trial. His professional opinion is that Sergio's best option is to submit a plea deal. I was elated to hear this. I said, "Wow, this is good news because then Vinni wouldn't have to testify, right?"

"Yes, that's correct. If Sergio pleads guilty to the charges as is, he would be sentenced to jail and would have to register as a sex offender for life. We will be setting another court date for September 12, which provides his attorney with time to review everything with him. If he does agree to change his plea, we will call you and Felipe in for a meeting to discuss the next steps. You will still have the opportunity to read a victim-witness statement even if there isn't a trial."

I saw Sergio's lawyer speak to him briefly over on his side of the courtroom, and then his lawyer exited. When they called Sergio's case, he walked over to the podium. The DA explained that the defense attorney was tied up with another case, and they agreed to schedule a compliance and election hearing for September 12. They gave Sergio a piece of paper with information on it. Another person who worked for the court stood up and said, "Sergio, you need to check in with probation downstairs before you leave." Sergio's probation says he can't be around people sixteen years of age or under without supervision. Becca's sister, at seventeen years old, is cutting it kind of close in my opinion. Why would a child support a pedophile in court?

Sergio and the circus exited the courtroom first. We waited a few minutes to give them a head start. Then we exited the courtroom. We spoke to the DA for a few minutes in the hallway. We told her we were really happy with the news from today and were excited to get back to our vacation. Vinni was spending the day with my family at the lake house in New Hampshire.

I updated my parents, Illianna, and Eric on what the DA had told me. "You guys! Sergio's lawyer is advising him to plead guilty. He has no defense!" We all walked down the stairs and out the front doors. As we were stepping out into the sunshine, we saw the entire Delgado circus waiting for us outside the courthouse. I just put my designer sunglasses on and walked right by them. Kiss my ass, bitches.

Our friend Eric wasn't as professional. He made a comment to Felipe Sr. that stirred the pot. He said, "You'd rather support a pedophile than your own son?" Felipe Sr. started swearing and told him to fuck off. I wasn't aware of this at the time, but I guess Eric also made a comment to Felipe Sr. as they were walking into the courtroom earlier on. A trial court officer told them to knock it off.

Ofelia videoed us leaving the courthouse that day, like the paparazzi. Doña Ofelia made a gesture to Felipe motioning to say, "you broke my heart." He just laughed in her face. Felipe Sr. called Eric a piece of vomit. They were hoping to provoke us and catch us doing something stupid on camera. We weren't the pissed off ones, though. We received good news that day.

I think Sergio's lawyer told him that very morning that his advice was to submit a plea deal. I'm sure his whole circus crew is pissed to hear the reality that they have no defense. Rotten fruit is falling down.

Suicide

The first person to bring up suicide during this ordeal was Ofelia, and it was at the family meeting. This was the first time Felipe, Trinny, D'Aven, and Illianna would be confronting her head on about what Sergio did. If I was there, I would have held a strong tone.

I was not there, but here's what I know. Carmen gathered her children and grandchildren. Estela joined her mother at this meeting. She was also the one who accompanied Sergio at the police station the day before, when he was questioned. Felipe went first and shared what Vinni had told him about Sergio. Ofelia and Estela seemed to accept this truth on some level. They cried and said they loved Vinni and all our kids.

Illianna went next. After she shared her truths, Ofelia asked, "Why didn't you tell me, Illianna? I helped raise you like you were my own!"

Illianna responded angrily and very honestly. "You weren't nice to me!" she said. "Your whole family was mean to me and made fun of my body. You gave me an eating disorder! If I told you, you probably wouldn't have believed me." She was only six years old. It's rare for a child to come forward about their sexual abuse. I read somewhere the average age of disclosure is an adult in their fifties.

D'Aven shared his truth after that. He was texting me updates at certain points during the meeting. He said at first Ofelia seemed genuinely upset about Sergio and seemed like she believed us. He was surprised by her reaction and expected her to be more defensive. The whole time the meeting was going on, Estela was texting someone. We all know it was Sergio, or someone next door at Gloria's house. She was giving them a play-by-play of the action.

Ofelia was sobbing at one point, falling to the ground, asking, "Why God? Why? I did the best I could with my kids. I should just kill myself!" If I were there, this is when I would have started clapping. Bravo, Ofelia. I would have went full asshole mode on her, encouraging her to kill herself.

Ofelia is not the victim in this story. There are four sexual abuse victims. Each of them carries this piece of their history with them forever. They have their own unique feelings, anxieties, and coping methods. We want justice and for Sergio to go to jail. We want him to register as a sex offender for life because this ensures he doesn't offend again, hopefully. But above that, we want our children to feel OK. We always want them to feel powerful. We never want them to feel like the bad thoughts are stronger than they are.

When Felipe came home from that family meeting, I demanded full disclosure of what went down. He said, "Surprisingly, Ofelia was not defensive. She cried and said she loved our kids. She said she was so sorry about Vinni."

"Ofelia believes the accusations to be true?" I was 100 percent skeptical right out the gate.

"That's what it seemed like. She was like, so over-the-top Ofelia though."

"Did you tell her to cut the shit and that you could see right through her?"

"Well, no. I mean, she said at one point she might commit suicide. I don't want that on my shoulders. She seems like she might choose to do the right thing. She did ask a ton of questions about court and jail. I didn't say shit about that though."

"Did you hug her?"

"Yeah, but—"

"I can't believe you hugged her! And who fucking cares if she commits suicide? That's not on anyone's shoulders but Sergio's. He is the bad person here that caused this mess!" I was so upset. I know everyone in this family greets each other affectionately, almost automatically, but if I was there, no way in hell I would have hugged an enabler.

"I wish I didn't hug her, but I did." I could tell Felipe empathized with my outrage, and I tried to empathize with his feelings too. For his whole life, these people were real family members to him. After a pause, Felipe continued his story. "When I was about to leave, my dad walked in. That's when I left. I cannot deal with him. He doesn't even know who Vinni is!"

"Oh my God! He just wants a front seat for the family drama. Why would he be involved in any of this?"

"I know, so fucked up right? Oh! And get this!" Felipe had more juicy details to share. "We told Ofelia she needs to talk to Mia and Gloria to make sure Sergio's not molesting Mia. She kind of just brushed that off. Then I asked her where Sergio was, and Ofelia goes 'oh, he's next door at Gloria's.'"

"Oh my God! He was next door the entire time? That is horrifying! Like what if he offered to 'put Mia to bed or something?' I want to vomit. The fucking nerve of that narcissistic asshole. The detective told him to stay away from us, and he purposely goes right next door the night you all have the family meeting? Wow."

Felipe went down to the courthouse the next day to file the restraining order. Trinny and Illianna went the day after that. Ofelia cried to Carmen, saying, "I'm worried Tonito will try to kill himself. He is so stressed out, Mami!"

Not only was Sergio not the victim, he was the Monster. If he or any of the Delgados want to leave this earth, it makes absolutely no difference to me, because to me, they are already dead.

Sergio probably can't even comprehend the amount of pain he has inflicted on our side of the tree. A dead Sergio cannot offend again. A dead Sergio would bring me peace.

I talk to all four of Sergio's victims. To them, I am mom or Titi. I hug them and tell them I love them often. I tell them they can be completely honest with me, and they do confide in me. Some of them struggle with their trauma on a daily basis. Some of them self-harm, and the cuts are visible. Some have suicidal thoughts and have utilized the crisis hotline. Some use substances to cope and suppress their pain. Some don't like talking about it, and some are more open with their feelings. Some lash out in anger and are triggered easily. The most important thing we are learning is that healing is a complicated process.

I am learning that there is no magical answer that will fix things. Buying Vinni a ton of clay stuff for his ninth birthday wasn't the perfect outlet for him. Just like drawing flowers can only do so much for me. Salem, Nacho, and Rosie are the absolute best, but purring kittens can't prevent triggering situations.

I also had my doubts about this plea deal thing, so I called the DA's office and asked our victim-witness advocate for more information. My therapist also strongly suggested that I tell her about how Ofelia and the circus waited for us outside the courtroom. Melanie was also concerned that both Ofelia and Becca are gun owners.

As I suspected, my victim-witness advocate did not feel any concern for my family regarding circus-clown gun ownership. She also said everyone has a right to be at court, and no one should be loitering outside. I asked if a trial court officer could stand outside if the other party did loiter again. She said that was unlikely. She then told me, "You don't need to be at court for these hearings, just Sergio does."

"I have to be there because I'm the mother of the victim in this case."

She responded with, "I understand." But I don't think she understands anything about what it's like to be me. She's younger than me, by about ten years probably. I doubt she has children of her own.

As the mother of the victim, I have murder dreams. I have anxiety attacks on vacation. I bail on plans last minute even if they're front row at the Red Sox. I can't finish all my work every day like I used to. I am still strong as fuck, but this trauma has changed me.

I don't like the system so far. I have no choice but to sit back and let the "justice" happen. There are no guarantees this criminal will go to jail. It's difficult for me to find peace during this time.

My victim-witness advocate has no idea why I need to be at every court date even though the law doesn't require it. She doesn't understand what this case means for my family.

She also explained the reality of this plea deal, which in itself is sobering as fuck. If he pleads guilty to the charges as is, he will be sentenced to jail time and will have to register as a sex offender for the rest of his life. She explained that is not the most likely scenario.

She gave an example of what might happen. "Sergio may plead guilty to the assault part, but not the indecent part. So then he may request one year of probation without jail time or registering as a sex offender. The charges will remain on his record though. Anyone looking would see the original charges and understand he submitted a plea deal." She further explained that if a plea deal were submitted, she and the prosecuting attorney would meet with Felipe and me to decide if it is something we will accept.

The thought of his lawyer advising him to change his plea felt so victorious at court back in July. Now that I'm receiving a more thorough explanation with a realistic scenario, it doesn't feel like it's going to be the answer we are looking for either. It seems like going to trial may be more than likely. This conversation also further solidified my understanding of the system—it had everything to do with the rights of criminals and nothing to do with supporting or protecting the victims.

I don't care who hates me for saying this. I wish Sergio was dead. Death is a desirable outcome either way.

Not Funny Haha,
Funny Weird

Today is August 24, 2022. My thirty-ninth birthday is next week. I woke up early this morning, at 5:30 a.m., just as Felipe was leaving for work. I felt like going on a rant after I saw an article on Facebook from Spectrum News 1 Worcester. The Spectrum News team said, "The US Department of Justice is allocating nearly $36 million in grants to ramp up local services and support for victims of sexual assault, including a nearly $681,000 grant to Massachusetts Department of Health." This triggered me. What exactly is the Massachusetts Department of Health going to do with that money for sexual assault victims? How will Vinni, Illianna, D'Aven, and Trevor access more services and support, with this funding?

Vinni has an actual case, and we are prosecuting Sergio, but we don't feel supported at all by the system. Illianna and D'Aven were told their cases weren't strong enough. They feel even less supported by this system. Trevor doesn't even feel like reporting his abuse is worth it. They are all victims of sexual assault, and they should be supported regardless, right? They have received nothing from the system.

The article says the money allocated to Massachusetts is being lauded by members of the state's congressional delegation. Do you know what lauded means? I did not, so I had to look it up. Lauded means highly praised or admired. The word lauded reminded me of the word laundered, so I was nervous for a moment.

Jim McGovern is a member of the United States House of Representatives, representing Massachusetts's second congressional district. In the article he says, "People live with this trauma for a long time and this money helps us support these victims dealing with some of the worst horrific, you know acts that we can imagine."

I actually have a funny story about Jim McGovern. Having worked at city hall, where McGovern's office is located, I know exactly who he is and what he looks like even though I've never actually talked to him directly. He is mostly bald but has this retaining wall of hair that goes around the bottom of his head. As a result, he appears to have a giant, endless forehead. He also wears glasses and has small, squinty eyes.

Last week we were at Martha's Vineyard. It's our favorite vacation spot, and we were there with my friend Kerri and her family. (She's the COVID-19 nurse I talked about earlier.) Anyways, we stayed in a rental house on Chappy Island because of my dumb ass. I booked it not realizing it was a ferry away from Edgartown and not actual Edgartown.

I think it was a Tuesday that we all decided to walk on the Chappy ferry and go shopping in Edgartown. We lost internet the night before at the rental house, and everyone was annoyed by that. The kids and I bought a ton of colored pencils, paper, and markers to bring back to our internet-less island house. While my family was waiting outside one of the shops, a man walked by who looked so familiar to me.

"Who is that guy, Felipe? Is it Jim McGovern?" This man had an endless forehead, a retaining wall of hair, glasses, and squinty eyes. Unfortunately, neither Felipe nor my friends knew who Jim McGovern was, so this Edgartown man's identity was not confirmed that day.

The weekend we came home from Martha's Vineyard, one of my favorite comedians, Chelsea Handler, posted some pictures from her family's stay on the Vineyard. I looked at the picture of her and her brother Roy, and I realized that it was Roy I saw that day in Edgartown, not Jim McGovern. Chelsea is lucky I thought her brother was a politician because if Kerri and I knew that was Roy Handler walking by, we would have been so annoying the rest of vacation trying to track Chelsea down and get her to join us for some dirty bananas at Nancy's.

Jim McGovern wasn't in Edgartown that day—it was a much cooler old man with an endless forehead and squinty eyes—but he did comment on this article saying this money will support victims who carry this horrific trauma for a long time. Ed Markey, another politician who is a Massachusetts senator, said, "These funds are vital for nonprofit providers across the Commonwealth of Massachusetts to ensure that survivors of sexual assault and violence have the resources they need to heal and thrive." I guess that's my answer. Nonprofit providers in Massachusetts will get this money.

Now that I've read the whole article, and laughed about thinking Roy Handler was Jim McGovern, I feel less rage in this moment. That headline jolted me, though, and it got me thinking.

Will the Massachusetts Children's Alliance (MACA) receive any trickle-down money from this grant? MACA is an accredited state chapter of the National Children's Alliance. According to their website, they "pioneer the most promising, leading-edge ways that help victims of child abuse receive the best possible care." I watched their video called "Child Abuse: Stars in the Field." I saw many familiar faces and names from the DA's office and MACA board.

Watching their video made me feel a bit angry and sad. They speak about the ins and outs of their days—the crazy stories they hear. My family's experience is more than a crazy story, and to be honest, we have never once felt supported by the DA's office, WPD, or MACA.

If you click on MACA's most recent newsletter, published in June 2022, you will see a banner a little way down that says, "Statewide Winner of OJJDP's Thirty-Ninth Annual Missing Children's Poster Contest." It then congratulates Olivia A, the Massachusetts winner.

Olivia found out about this poster contest before Thanksgiving. It was before our lives changed forever, before our family tree split in half. She was nominated by her fifth-grade class to enter this contest because they unanimously voted her as the best artist in her grade. I helped her fill out the application, and at the time, the Office of Juvenile Justice and Delinquency Prevention (OJJDP) was a government agency that had nothing to do with my family. Additionally, the Massachusetts Children's Alliance didn't hold much weight either. It was just a contest my little artist wanted to enter.

Olivia immediately started brainstorming for her poster. Her drawing had to convey the message "Bring Our Missing Children Home." Her concept was actually quite powerful. It features a crying mother standing outside her home and a lost, lonely child illuminated by a streetlight in a far-off city.

By the time the winner was announced at the end of April, I had forgotten all about the poster and was dealing with the actual agencies instead. It was one month after Sergio had been arraigned in court. Olivia's teacher announced to her class that she had some news to share about Olivia. She started reading from an official letter. "This is from the Massachusetts Children's Alliance and the Office of Juvenile Justice and Delinquency Prevention." Hearing these words jolted Olivia. She thought her teacher might speak about the trauma her family was going through. She heard the words Juvenile and Justice frequently at home, never in a positive context. Once her teacher got further into the letter and Olivia realized she was the state winner, she was ecstatic.

I'm so proud of Olivia. Dyslexia makes reading and math a struggle for her, but her artistic abilities are unmatched. I also find it incredibly odd that my daughter is MACA's literal poster child, featuring her artwork in their marketing materials, yet my son, the actual sexual abuse victim, feels zero support from the organization. That's why I think this shit is not funny haha, funny weird.

Impossibilities

Impossibility is the state or fact of being impossible. It is an impossible thing or situation. Today I'm writing about the impossibilities I feel.

We went to court on September 12 for Sergio's compliance and election hearing. The DA said that Sergio is still considering a plea deal. When I expressed my concern about him pleading guilty to a lesser, lamer crime, she said, "They've been talking about the actual charges, so it would mean jail time and sex offender registration." We were also assigned a new victim-witness advocate that day.

One of the trial court officers was a guy I went to high school with. I wonder if he knows my case or just hears what happens in court. It's impossible for us to go to court without seeing someone we know. The next court date is called "final compliance hearing" and is scheduled for December 7. If Sergio keeps his plea of not guilty, a trial date will be set at this court hearing.

A few days ago, I emailed our new victim-witness advocate asking if she could gauge when the trial date would be set. She said, "It would be impossible for me to guess! We not only have to take the prosecutor and defense attorney's schedules into account, but also the court calendar, your schedule, as well as that of the defendant, with the two attorneys being of most importance—since they already have other trials on their calendars."

Basically, it's impossible to know when the trial would be set. Could be early next year, late next year, the following year, who knows. December 7, 2022 is just six days before the anniversary of when Vinni spoke his truth. December 13, 2022 will mark one year of living with the truth for me. Waiting for this trial feels impossible. It's so easy for Sergio to delay and deflect. They could set a trial date for two years from now, and the day it starts, Sergio could change his plea to guilty, and then we wait again for sentencing. It's impossible for me to feel peace right now.

So, I did something controversial today. I created a TikTok account called RottenFruit22. I posted a video using a screenshot from one of Becca's latest videos. It's a photo of her and Sergio. I added text to the photo and created a short slideshow. It says:

This is Sergio Delgado. He is twenty-five years old. He is married to Becca Delgado.

He was arraigned in Worcester District Court on March 24, 2022, for two counts of indecent assault and battery on a minor under fourteen years of age.

He was released on personal recognizance and is not allowed to be around children under the age of sixteen unsupervised.

He is due back in court on December 7, 2022, for final compliance before the trial date is set.

Four victims have come forward so far.

It felt good to air that out. To announce his crimes. My family members, who suffered alongside me during this process, cheered me when I shared this video. His arraignment should have been posted for the public. I'm just doing what the newspaper should be doing. Some of my friends, however, think this might give his defense attorney ammunition to use against us at trial. That I suck at making TikToks? I am definitely guilty of that.

It's impossible for my friends or anyone not in my shoes to really understand what my life is like. How taking the high road, or being mature, or holding back—being completely, perfectly behaved—guarantees nothing. Sometimes, to put yourself first and for feelings of justice, you just do the petty, loud thing anyways. Today is the day I ran out of fucks completely and posted the truth.

My intentions with this video are threefold: to alert the public that he is an unsafe individual; to encourage Sergio to plead guilty now; and to transfer the shame. Living in peace will be impossible for Sergio going forward, not my family.

Curveballs

Felipe texted me this morning saying his day was going well. He had a great crew, and things were going smoothly. I was happy for him. He had been having a tough time at work lately. As the foreman, he is responsible for a lot of things and people at the jobsite. Sometimes the fabricator sends the wrong materials. Or sends them on the wrong day before another trade finishes their piece of construction. Or the design doesn't actually work in real life. Or sometimes weather delays their progress. All these things had been putting pressure on him, and it was nice to hear he felt better, like he had a good handle on the day.

Then he texted me saying he just got thrown a curveball. One of the guys on his crew came in late and was completely fucked up on drugs. He was swaying back and forth on his feet. His eyes were half open and closing, like he was having a hard time staying awake. Felipe knew he was a liability and sent him home.

I got to my office after dropping the kids off at school, and then the craziest thing happened to me! Another curveball, if you will. My office is located in an old brick building that is three stories high. I'm up on the third floor at the end of the hallway. I love my office. It has two rooms; one is large, where my workspace and meeting area are. The other is smaller, with a gold couch and teal minifridge. This one is my break room, also the room my kids like to hang out in when they're at work with me. It also has a very large, old window—the kind with rope in it. I've never opened this window before, until today.

That morning, when I opened my office door, I heard birds freaking out. This is normal though; I always hear birds in my office. They made nests in the vents, and I hear them all the time. But this was nuts! There was a small bird trapped in the window! It was stuck between the screen and the windowpane. Like how on earth did you get in there, little birdy? I had to set it free, but I absolutely did not want that thing flying into the rest of my office.

I pulled the couch over to the windowsill. I needed to stand on this in order to reach the big window and push it open. While I was climbing up, the bird flew to the top of the window. This was a good thing. I said, "OK, little birdy, I'm going to help you. Please do not touch me. Do not bite me. Stay right up there until I get the screen open." I got the windowpane open enough to reach my hands in and open the screen a few inches. Then I closed the windowpane. "OK, birdy. You know what to do now!" A few seconds later, the bird flew out. I closed the screen, shut the window, and moved the couch back.

I didn't see any rips in the screen. I have no idea how that bird got trapped in there, but I'm glad it's free now. There was another bird on the outside of the window freaking out while I was working on freeing the stuck one. They were missing their friend.

Apparently, someone else was missing someone that day. That afternoon, Felipe received a text from his mother, Carmen. It was a Facebook meme that read, "No soy una madre perfecta...Hijo te amo, y aunque no sea perfecta, pero mi amor por ti es perfecto." This translates to, "I am not a perfect mother...Son I love you, and even though I'm not perfect, my love for you is perfect." Another curveball for Felipe. This was the first time he had heard from his mother since that last call with Carmen. He forwarded the message to me. I called him to talk about it.

"So how do you feel about this?" I asked him.

"I don't know, man, what the fuck!" He laughed a little because we had been going back and forth all day with these crazy stories, and now here was his mom, making contact with him after three months of not speaking, smack in the middle of his workday.

I said, "Do you want to talk to her about it?"

"No. I don't know. I don't want her to think things are OK just because she sends a random Facebook meme."

"Yeah. That meme doesn't make anything OK. You can be honest with her about that. Tell her how you don't feel her love or support right now. It's not up to you to do anything to fix this. It's up to her."

"I don't think I want to even talk to her. I don't want to disrupt my peace my right now."

"I get that too." I support Felipe either way because it's his mom, and it's his relationship. I've told my kids the same. They know they can call Nana or write her a letter if they choose to. They miss her so much. I told Felipe, "You can marinate in the positive part of this—that your mom is missing you and is thinking about you. I think she knows she's done something wrong. She might not be ready to face it or fix it, but she does love and miss you. You can decide later if you want to talk to her or respond. Protecting your peace right now is a good choice."

Maybe sometimes when life throws a curveball at you, the best option is to jump out of the way, so you don't get hit.

The next day, September 29, 2022, made me realize I started writing this book exactly three months ago. It dawned on me today that I started writing this book three days after our last call with Carmen. Felipe told me yesterday he wants to send it to her to read.

I haven't sent the book yet, but today I acted impulsively. I texted Carmen the TikTok about Sergio and his charges. Then I texted her. I said, "Hi, Carmen. I feel really badly about how our last conversation ended. My whole family, including me, loves you and misses you very much. We want you to be in our life, but we need to make sure you are ready to cut Ofelia out of your life. She is not family, she is an abuser."

I have no expectations that she will respond. She has not responded to anything I have texted her since January. She doesn't just dodge curveballs; Carmen doesn't swing at anything I'm pitching. I think she is afraid of Ofelia. Carmen says she depends on Ofelia, but from my point of view, Ofelia benefits from controlling Carmen.

I remember during the interim period, when we were waiting for the police to question Sergio, Carmen told me she felt a lot of anxiety. She said she wanted to schedule an appointment with her therapist and ask her to prescribe another dose of her antianxiety medication. I said yes, you should call and do that! But Carmen hesitated. She chose not to call her doctor out of fear. Ofelia drives her to her doctor appointments, and Ofelia picks up her medications, and Ofelia would ask Carmen for an explanation as to why she was feeling anxious.

In the past, Carmen would lie about visiting with my family. It stems from Ofelia being a pain in the ass and trying to control people. It was easier for Carmen to say, "Oh just going to see Poncho's nephew," instead of saying she was coming to my house.

It was back when we were living at our old house on Swan Ave, and I think I was pregnant with Olivia at the time. I invited

Carmen and Poncho over for dinner that night and said it would be ready at six. I was making some kind of baked fish, but I forget what the side dishes were. Six came and went, and soon it was close to seven. I asked Felipe if he had heard from his parents, and he said no. I was keeping the food warm in the oven until they arrived.

Carmen and Poncho finally showed up around seven, and Ofelia was with them, which was a surprise. Ofelia complained about my fish being dried out. I agreed the fish was dry, but I was also planning on serving it an hour earlier. Ofelia was at Carmen and Poncho's house when they said they had plans to eat dinner at my house. Not being included made Ofelia feel jealous, so she did everything she could to delay their departure, making them late to my dinner. She also invited herself to come along.

Going to visit Poncho's nephew doesn't set Ofelia off like that. She doesn't immediately stall Carmen from going or invite herself, so that's why Carmen would lie.

From what I hear from Trinny and her kids, Carmen does not talk about us or Sergio with Ofelia. According to them, whenever Carmen speaks to Ofelia, there is a big fat elephant in the room that never gets brought up.

What's the point of having a fake relationship with an abuser, where you have to lie to keep the peace and walk on eggshells? Felipe and I wonder about what Christmas Eve will be like this year. Will this be our first Christmas without Nana and

Grampa in our life? Or will we reconcile in time for Christmas at Trinny's?

Felipe's side of the family is good at dodging curveballs. My family, on the other hand, is good at throwing them. My mother called a few days ago and said they were planning to go to Arizona for Christmas. This made me feel sad, and having to tell my kids this news made me feel even sadder. We had been bracing ourselves for Felipe's side of the family, but we did not see this curveball coming from my parents.

My brother said they wanted to come home for Christmas this year, but they had been having issues finding a dogsitter for their dog, Teddy. My mom asked if them going to Arizona for Christmas would make me mad, and I said no. She explained how she hasn't seen Mikey and the kids in over nine months, so they really wanted to go out there. She also felt bad about Teddy, my brother's neurotic dog. He had issues. They have a couple dogsitters out there that he's done well with, but they weren't having any luck finding someone who would be available to watch the dog during the holidays.

So my mom and dad decided they would go out to Arizona for Christmas to be with Mikey and his family. I told Felipe the news, and his response, "What the fuck? We're low on parents this year!" I know the kids will have a similar reaction.

I just want to put this out into the universe—we are sick of curveballs, and we're ready to hit the jackpot.

Transferring the Shame

I talked about my TikTok account with my therapist, Melanie. By that point I had four videos up.

The second video I made starts with a school worksheet, colored by Vinni, that says, "Your body is YOUR BODY! That's so important that I think we should say it again: It's YOUR BODY." The next two slides are photos of Sergio's face with the words: "This is from a third-grade sex education class. Sex education teaches kids about consent. Opting out helps sexual predators."

The third video I posted starts with a picture of a book written by a nine-year-old girl named Jessie. It's called "Please Tell!" It's a child's story about sexual abuse. The next slides are Sergio's face with the words: "Safe adults believe children when they say something important. Safe adults don't ask kids to keep secrets. Safe adults don't isolate children."

The fourth video I posted starts with the BACA logo. The next two slides are Sergio's face with the words: "Bikers Against Child Abuse exists to empower and protect children. No child deserves to live in fear. They will surround a child in court while they testify so the perpetrator will not intimidate them."

My fifth video was "removed for violating community guidelines." I also got banned from posting on TikTok until October 8. I am in TikTok jail for speaking the truth. I suspect the enablers were the ones who reported me to the TikTok police. This video starts with a picture of Sergio and Becca on their wedding day standing in front of the bridge at Elm Park, along with Tony, Ofelia, Gloria, Estela, Mia, Russ and Lynn (Becca's parents), and Becca's sister. I put stickers over the children's faces to block them out. The word "ENABLERS" was written at the bottom. The next slides zoom in on Tony and Ofelia's faces with the words: "An enabler is an individual who knows sexual abuse is occurring and does nothing. Their loyalties to the perpetrator put them at odds with preventing sexual abuse."

Later on that morning, after I posted that last video, I saw a post in the "now" section. I am an older millennial and technologically challenged. I don't understand this part of TikTok, so I did not view or click on the video, especially when I saw the name "Gen. Russ." I immediately thought it might be Becca's dad, and the profile picture did resemble him.

This morning I also noticed that Becca's TikTok account is now private. That made me feel really good. Like I slapped my hand across her mouth. The last video I saw that she posted was one of Sergio and her seventeen-year-old sister cuddling, all snuggly on the couch. In another one, Becca is sitting in the back of a cop car saying, "If touching my family's butts becomes illegal, lock me up." She also posted Sergio's fresh haircut the day before he had court.

Now everybody knows why he has to go court and who is supporting him. I don't think Becca's parents, Russ and Lynn, appreciated the shout-out. Becca's parents not only support their son-in-law, they brought a seventeen-year-old girl, their daughter, to court to support him. Why don't they take these charges seriously, and why aren't they committed to protecting children?

Would Russ and Lynn believe their own child if they said they were being abused? It's scary to think about it. The person their child married is suddenly in trouble, big trouble, with two counts of child molestation charges. What story did Sergio tell to convince them that these allegations are false or untrue? What did he say or do to win their support?

Has Sergio discussed his attorney's advice with them to plead guilty? That hasn't altered their opinion? His own attorney says there's no good defense strategy based on what the DA got against him. It's hard to gauge what they know because the Delgados lie constantly, about everything.

All we know is that Becca's parents support a sexual predator, and they don't protect their teenage daughter from him. We carry Sergio's trauma with us forever. We didn't choose him as family; he was an evil spawn. Becca chose him to be her family, and she can choose to leave him when she's had enough.

It feels good speaking our truth even if it is "teetering on the fence of libel." I like to call it transferring the shame. These people should feel ashamed of themselves for supporting a pedophile, but they should be downright mortified for not protecting their own child. A safe person would establish strong boundaries with a family member who was on probation, not allowed to be alone with children.

Melanie, my therapist, didn't have much to say about my videos. She said she doesn't have an opinion either way. She asked what my goals were in posting them and expressed concern about possible backlash. I shared my reasons and said, yeah I do worry about backlash a little, but ultimately, it feels good to air it out.

It feels really good knowing I shut Becca up. It will feel even better if Sergio loses her family's support entirely.

The shame is being transferred to those who continue to support and enable abusers. The survivors will not carry this weight. I know my stunt is working because Guera535, aka Ofelia, just viewed my videos. Shame, shame, shame, I know your name.

Criminal Harassment

It was Friday, October 28, 2022. I made plans to pick Illianna up from college that afternoon. It was such a beautiful drive up to New England College. The fall foliage, bright blue sky, and old New England buildings made the hour and forty minute drive up route 77 quite enjoyable.

I checked out her dorm room when I arrived and said hello to Lyanny, her roommate and longtime bestie. We loaded her laundry into my trunk, and she said, "I have so much to tell you, Titi. I practically have a boyfriend!" I laughed as she told me all her college stories. We stopped for sushi in Leominster when we were about halfway home. We ordered the rainbow roll, golden roll, sexy lady roll, and salmon sushi.

Right as we were finishing our dinner, Felipe texted me. He said, "I couldn't wait, I had to open it." Next, he sent a picture of court paperwork with my name, Erin Arvizu, listed as the defendant and the name Sergio Delgado listed as the plaintiff. Sergio is trying to charge me with criminal harassment. I have to go before the clerk magistrate on December 7—the same day as his court hearing. If the clerk decides I am in fact a criminal, my case will go before a judge. The paperwork says I can bring witnesses and share my side. It also says that Sergio, as the complainant, has to be present, or else my case could be dismissed. He can also bring witnesses and share his side. Are we really going to hash this out in front of the clerk, then move on to courtroom 15 to hear when his trial date is set?

On the paperwork, it says the date of offense for the criminal harassment was on January 13, 2022. On January 13, we had been living with Vinni's truth for one month. The police had just questioned Sergio two days before. The family meeting at Carmen's house had just taken place the night before. Ofelia had just sobbed in front of her family as she heard about Sergio's crimes, and she begged for forgiveness. I posted a meme on my Facebook page on January 13 that said, "Never seek revenge, rotten fruit falls by itself." There was no reference as to what was actually going on in my personal life—at that time, this was just a vague, cryptic Facebook post. I messaged Becca on January 13 saying, "Hi, Becca, we filed a restraining order against your husband today. I don't know what Sergio has told you about what's been going on, but if you want to talk to me, you can call me, 508-XXX-XXXX."

I also texted Gloria on January 13, saying, "Gloria do not let that fucking pervert near your kids. You are a good mom, and you need to protect your girls. You cannot trust him." Gloria never responded to this text message. Becca didn't respond to me either and unfriended me on Facebook. Sergio unfriended me and blocked me. Estela unfriended and blocked me. I then unfriended Gloria and Ofelia. On February 2, Mia, Gloria's daughter, tried calling me through Instagram one night, persistently. She called over and over again, four or five times in a row. I did not answer, but I messaged her. I asked, "Mia, are you safe? Stay away from your Uncle Sergio. He abuses kids in our family." She was only six years old at the time, in first grade, so I'm not sure if she could read that message or not.

On June 29, 2022, three days after that last call with Carmen, I found my original post from January 13, and I added a screenshot of one of Sergio's posts. It's a picture of him holding his big-ass gun, saying, "For you, Mother Russia." I posted this screenshot in the comments under the Rotten Fruit meme. I added the caption "Rotten Fruit" to the picture. This was also the day I started writing this book. I'm not harassing him. I'm processing what he did to my family, out loud, because it protects more kids than staying silent. Sergio sexually assaulted four of his cousins, causing lifelong trauma to our family—do you think I'm committing a misdemeanor by speaking out about it?

I don't really know what to do next or how I should respond. I emailed a copy of the paperwork to my victim-witness advocate at the DA's office. I also researched civil suits and found an attorney that specializes in representing cases like ours. Prosecuting at the state level gets jail time and sex offender registry. Filing a civil suit goes after financial assets. It's not something I really thought about much before because I just wanted to be done with the whole court thing. But now I'm considering it.

The attorney I found is named Carmen, such a coincidence right? I'm going to wait and see if the DA responds and then contact the attorney for a consultation. In the meantime, I texted my friends and family about the harassment charges. Several people suggested I shut the fuck up for now and not post anything further. One friend said to do the complete opposite, contact the press and go nuts.

Part of me wants to be a dick and post the charges on social media saying, guess who also has court on December 7? But I'm not going to. I'm sticking to my plan of talking to the DA and then contacting the civil suit attorney. What does freedom of speech really mean though? If someone commits crimes against my family and me, I should be free to speak about it.

The next night, Saturday, October 29, was the big Halloween party—something Vinni had been looking forward to. Nolan is his best friend and the host of the party. Our whole family had been invited. Olivia had her last softball game that night too. I asked my youngest daughter, "Do you want to go to Livi's softball game or to the party?" Luna said she wanted to go to the party. Vinni immediately lost his mind, and a huge outburst ensued.

"No! Luna cannot come! This is not fair! No!" Vinni yelled as he stormed upstairs to his room. Everything spiraled out of control from that point on. There was nothing Felipe or I could do to alleviate the situation. Felipe brought Liv to softball. I continued trying to talk to Vinni. I explained how Luna going to the party wouldn't ruin everything because there would be tons of other kids for her to play with. I said, "If anything, Luna being there will give Nolan's little brother a buddy to play with, and then neither of them will bother you and Nolan." Nothing was working. He wouldn't open his bedroom door.

I hate when we end up here. I worry about him self-harming. I feel heartbroken for his anger and sadness. Through the closed door I said, "Vinni, what are you doing? I worry that you might be cutting your arm. I need to make sure you're safe."

Through his anger and the tears, he said to me, "For your information, Mom, I have not self-harmed for over a week!" I started crying when he said this. I also told him I was really proud of him. Not just for not self-harming, but also for telling me. I thanked him for sharing that with me. I told him I know it was hard for him to go a whole week without doing it, so I think he's really strong for making it.

At one point, little Luna, who is a tiny five-year-old, walked up to Vinni's door and said to her brother, "Vinni you can just pretend I don't exist." It was hard to understand her last word because she started crying. She knows Vinni is hurt. She knows he takes a lot of anger out on her. It's not fair to her. But here she is, trying to sacrifice herself to help her brother feel better.

Felipe came back home after dropping Livi off. He tried talking to Vinni some more. I was dressed head to toe in my Medusa costume not knowing what the fuck to do. Vinni wants to stay home. Luna wants to go to the party and has already been bundled up in three layers under her witch costume to keep her warm. Felipe has to go to the softball game. If I stay home with Vinni, Luna has to stay home too. I told Vinni he had to go to the game or to the party. If he went to the game, he could wait in the car to try to relax and calm down. He didn't exactly choose the game, but he went with Felipe so he didn't have to be at the party with Luna.

The party looked really fun because the decorations were insane, and everybody was in good spirits, but I couldn't really have fun because I was carrying Vinni's sadness with me. Why does he have so much animosity toward Luna? Why does he need to manipulate and control the situation whenever our family has plans? Why do his emotions go from zero to one thousand over the smallest, slightest inconvenience? Why can't I keep my fucking mouth shut on social media?

Because of Sergio Anthony Delgado. It's SAD. SAD as fuck.

What qualifies as criminal harassment in Massachusetts? MA General Laws, chapter 265, section 43A, states, "Whoever willfully and maliciously engages in a knowing pattern of conduct or series of acts over a period of time directed at a specific person, which seriously alarms that person and would cause a reasonable person to suffer substantial emotional distress, shall be guilty of the crime of criminal harassment and shall be punished by imprisonment in a house of correction for not more than 2.5 years or by a fine of not more than $1,000, or by both such fine and imprisonment." For the record, what Sergio did to Vinni sounds exactly like criminal harassment. Malice indicates the intention without justification. Sergio can't justify what he did to Vinni. Legally, a "reasonable person" denotes a person who is essentially intelligent enough and has enough good judgment to function within a society that protects their own interest and the interests of others. By definition, Sergio is not a reasonable person, nor are his family members.

What is indecent assault and battery in Massachusetts? MA General laws, chapter 265, section 13B states, "An indecent assault and battery is an intentional and unjustified touching of a private area, including, but not limited to, the breast, abdomen, thigh, buttocks, genital or pubic areas of a male or female. Whoever commits indecent assault and battery on a child under the age of 14 shall be punished by imprisonment in the state prison for not more than 10 years, or by imprisonment in the house of correction for not more than 2.5 years." I have been told by the DA that Sergio is facing up to five years for his two counts. I don't fully understand why he's not facing two ten-year sentences. But now, here I am potentially facing 2.5 years in prison and a fine of $1,000.

This is quite interesting, right? Touching a child's private parts can get you 2.5 years in prison. Talking about the perpetrator touching a child's private parts can get you 2.5 years in prison and a $1,000 fine. Talking is worse than touching—is this really the reality we live in? Or will the clerk and the DA and everyone else see this as complete bullshit?

I don't believe I have committed criminal harassment by posting about Sergio on social media. I have not called, texted, emailed, or contacted Sergio. Nor have I ever threatened him in any way. I have announced his crimes through Rotten Fruit social media accounts, and I've shared things on my personal accounts. I am processing my family's trauma out loud because it helps me feel better. Being silent makes me feel worse, and it helps Sergio feel better. Being silent shouldn't be the standard anymore.

I wonder if Sergio's attorney encouraged him to file these charges. Does this help him defend Sergio? Does my big mouth make Sergio less guilty? I am curious about the January 13 date as my offense date. If anything, I started causing trouble in September when I launched the Rotten Fruit TikTok. And then again in October when I landed myself in TikTok jail.

It's not criminal harassment you dicks—it's transferring the shame.

Never Have I Ever

Never have I ever held a real, loaded gun, so I sure as fuck have never fired one, nor do I intend to. I don't like guns, and I've never felt the need to own one or learn to shoot. Being a small person, I would never get physically aggressive with anyone because I am quite literally smaller than a fifth grader. Doing research about criminal harassment is interesting. I am mostly finding advice for defending stalking, sexual assault, domestic violence, etc. Not a lot of people are talking about what to do if you get charged with criminal harassment for speaking about the family pedophile. On the Massachusetts website, among the examples of criminal harassment, I found Sergio's crime in the list. Sexually assaulting someone, especially routinely like he did for four years, is criminal harassment.

In terms of my own criminal harassment charges, I received a response from the DA's office that Monday. My victim-witness advocate said, "Hi Erin, Sorry to hear this and I did speak to the prosecutor about it. The defense is saying that there have been some instances of FB posts and that would possibly cause them to file this. It would be best to not mention these charges/case on social media platforms. We have no say in harassment/restraining orders and do not represent you in this hearing."

Roger that, DA. I am on my fucking own with this thing. I also spoke to that law office I mentioned earlier. Becca is no dummy—well, in a literal book smart sense, she is not. She is an accountant who used to work at a bank. She homesteaded that shit, to protect her principal residence from civil suit back in April when they purchased their home. This means filing a civil suit is not a viable option as Sergio doesn't have any assets to recover anything financially.

The woman I spoke with at this office was incredibly understanding and helpful and honest. I asked her briefly about my situation with the harassment charges and she said to go before the magistrate, see what they say, and if it moves to a case before a judge, to call and they can refer me to another attorney. I thanked her. Then I formulated my plan.

All the information I have at this point, on Wednesday, November 2, is that my date of offense is January 13, 2022, and my charge is criminal harassment, and that it possibly has to do with some Facebook posts. I started organizing my thoughts and created an actual timeline of events. I am not an attorney. I am a broken, strong-ass mother standing up for my family against evil, just like I have been doing this whole time, but I must be so careful about what I say in court. I do not want to make anything worse. But never have I ever, Your Honor, criminally harassed someone.

Court Timeline—note to self: say as little as possible.

December 13, 2022: My son, Vinni, tells me his cousin Sergio has been sexually abusing him for four years.

Interim period: Illianna, D'Aven come forward; we file all applicable reports with police, DA, DCF, etc.

January 11, 2022: Trinny has a missed call from Sergio. We later found out this was the day Sergio was questioned by police. At the station, the police questioned him about sexually assaulting Vinni, D'Aven, and Illianna. The police tell Sergio to stay away from us.

January 12, 2022: A family meeting takes place at Carmen's house at 32 Arthur Street.

January 13, 2022: Felipe, my husband, filed a restraining order against Sergio to keep him away from us and our home.

At this point in time, on January 13, my family and Trinny's family were still figuring out the charges and who would be moving forward with cases. Sergio was told to stay away, but he didn't, and Sergio had access to twelve guns. The detective also told us that based on his responses, Sergio displayed traits of a sociopath and not that of your average child molester. Sergio had danger written all over him at this time, yet he is accusing me of criminally harassing him.

This is where I should stop talking when I'm at court, maybe a few lines higher, maybe not every detail, but this is my guide for what has happened. I also want to have a complete factual account of all events, so I'm continuing the timeline below up to December 7 to have in my folder, just in case.

January 13, 2022: I posted that Rotten Fruit meme as a tiny expression of what I was going through.

February 10, 2022: Sergio was formally charged with two counts of indecent assault and battery on a minor under fourteen years old. This is the start of Vinni's case. This is also the day I filed a report with DCF for Mia being groomed/molested. And reported one more tidbit of information that Vinni disclosed—that Sergio would use his cell phone during the abuse. There was zero reaction from the DA or police about my son being exploited, and they refused to search his phone.

February 18, 2022: Ofelia and Estela file restraining orders against Trevor. He is kicked out of his home because he lives at the same address as the Delgados, 32 Arthur Street. Trevor moves into my house with my family.

March 24, 2022: Sergio is arraigned in court for two counts of indecent assault and battery on a minor under fourteen years.

April 1, 2022: Carmen lists 32 Arthur Street. for sale. The property is under contract very quickly and with tenant agreements in place. Carmen was set to move out and into her new condo in early June. Trinny was set to close toward the end of June. The plan with Trevor was he would stay with us until Trinny moved to her new house.

During this time, Ofelia made life a living hell for Trinny and her family. Ofelia would burn enough sage and incense in the hallway to set off the fire alarms upstairs at Trinny's house on the third floor. These literal fire alarms at all hours of the day and night traumatized not just the adults living there, but especially little four-year-old Je'Nise. She would be startled randomly by the fire alarm and cry and feel so scared. Trinny would find these ritualistic incense/sage piles burning in the stairwell of the hallway.

One time, Trinny had had enough of Ofelia's torment and just whipped a whole bucket of water down the stairs, extinguishing the flames and soaking both staircases all the way down to the first floor. Carmen got mad at her for doing that. Trinny said, "Um, hello, talk to your other daughter about why she's burning shit in the hallway!"

June 20, 2022: Trinny and her family move to their new home, away from the abusive Delgados.

June 26, 2022: I start to lose hope that things with Carmen will ever be OK again. Sergio ruined our relationship with Carmen.

June 29, 2022: I started writing down my story—as a way to process what we had just gone through and understand how we got to this point. It was therapeutic to organize my thoughts in an orderly, thoughtful way that told our story. I also named the main character in my story, Sergio Delgado, as Rotten Fruit on this day.

July 19, 2022: At Sergio's compliance hearing, his attorney told the DA he is advising Sergio to plead guilty.

This was when the Delgados waited for us outside the courthouse and videoed us as we exited. Eric happened to bump into a friend in courtroom 15 that day...dealing with her own case. Anyhoo, she saw Ofelia and the gang waiting and getting their cameras ready as we were about to exit.

September 12, 2022: At this compliance hearing, the DA said that Sergio was strongly considering pleading guilty to the full charges, per his attorney's advice. A final compliance hearing was set for December 7.

September 22, 2022: The first day of fall. I create Rotten Fruit TikTok and start to share my story with an intense purpose that protects children. Being silent makes Sergio and his supporters more comfortable, but in reality, it puts kids at risk because more people are likely to trust him. Letting people know that Sergio is unsafe will make more people aware and less likely to grant him access to their children.

October 7, 2022: I create the Rotten Fruit Facebook account. Each expansion of me releasing pieces of my story in the way that I choose is freeing. It hurts questionable people's feelings, but it does more to protect children than staying silent does.

October 19, 2022: I shared the Rotten Fruit post on my personal Facebook timeline, announcing Sergio as an unsafe person. People are now discovering for the first time my connection to Rotten Fruit profiles even though they don't fully understand the role I play or my relationship to Sergio's victims.

October 26, 2022: I shared another Rotten Fruit post on my timeline, asking my Facebook friends how they would respond to a child if they disclosed sexual abuse to them. This was the post with the children's book written by nine-year-old Jessie. Every child deserves countless safe adults in their life who protect them and care for them. Unsafe adults are tricky to see sometimes, especially when they are your nephew or uncle or father or brother or friend.

This was also the day that Sergio and/or his attorney filed criminal harassment charges against me, the broken, strong-ass mother.

October 28, 2022: I received the letter in the mail with the limited information about my alleged crime.

November 2, 2022: I stay calm. I continue to prepare. I also brace myself for curveballs because it's barely November and we have a whole ass month to go before court.

December 7, 2022: We go to court with crystals in pockets, armed with my timelines and evidence and hope for the best. I guess I'm up first, then we do Sergio's thing?

As I reviewed my timeline, I started to see the pattern of retaliation by the Delgados. Whenever their life becomes heated, they retaliate. Sergio was charged with child molestation charges, so they kicked Trevor out of his home. Carmen sold the three decker and Trinny bought a new house, so they made life a literal burning, smoky hell until they moved away for good. I start sharing my story about the trauma Sergio has caused to my family, and he charges me with criminal harassment. Sergio has a court date on December 7? The Delgados make sure Erin Arvizu has one too.

The more I think about criminal harassment and this timeline of events, I am realizing that both Sergio and Ofelia have committed criminal harassment. Ofelia's routine smoke stunt to set off fire alarms is 100 percent criminal harassment. Sergio never got the opportunity to sexually abuse Je'Nise, so Ofelia traumatized her in another way. She learned from the best, remember—Doña Ofelia was the one who first taught her that cruelty toward children is 100 percent acceptable.

I might be a blunt-ass bitch, but never have I ever behaved like a Delgado.

Interim Period

This is the period I refer to, from December 13, 2021, to January 11, 2022. This month was extremely emotionally exhausting. It was stressful as fuck for my family, Trinny's family, and Carmen. We were all coming to terms with the abuse and the predator, but we had to pretend things were fine around the Delgados because the police hadn't yet questioned him.

Monday, December 13, started off interesting. I woke up after having a dream about Taylor Swift playing a show on Martha's Vineyard, and I was in a long line waiting to see her. I also talked to Felipe about how I was waking up like five times a night sweating and how I'd been exhausted. I thought I was just getting over COVID-19 or maybe some premenopausal shit was fucking with me. Now I see that my physical body was warning me about something my mind had yet to comprehend. Vinni told me his truth that night.

On Tuesday, December 14, I told Felipe our kids will never go to 32 Arthur Street again, and he agreed. I said Carmen, Poncho, and Trinny's family could come here, but we would never ever go to 32 Arthur again. I said I would make a Saran Wrap ball for Christmas since my kids loved that in the past, and we would create new traditions this year. I told Vinni I was proud of him for telling me and I wished I had known years ago so I could have protected him.

I felt so much anger. The betrayal. The outrage over what my son had been through. It was so strong and heavy and intense and overwhelming.

I asked Reilly that morning if she had a crazy busy day or if she could talk. I said I needed some advice. She said to call around 9:15 a.m., and I did. I talked to her for about an hour. She explained the process and supported me while I shared my story and cried. I told her, "Thank you, Reilly! Just talking to you about this gives me so much hope and direction. I appreciate you so much."

I spoke to the social worker at the pediatrician's office. I then left a voicemail with the WPD detective bureau. I also spoke to DCF, and they said they were referring the case to the DA for criminal charges. DCF said we should tell other family members so they could keep their kids away. I even suggested possibly contacting Gloria right away, for Mia's sake.

That night Felipe went to 32 Arthur Street to tell Carmen and Trinny.

On Wednesday, December 15, Trinny and I made plans to meet at WPD at 11:00 a.m. I spoke to the DA's office and scheduled the SANE interview. This was the day I told my mom. After talking with police, I texted Felipe, "OK so we filed the police report. The next step is for Vinni to go to that interview next week. The DA and police use that to establish which charges to bring him up on, then they arrest him. They will tell us when they are arresting him."

I also texted him this: "The lady at the DA said it is best if we don't ask Vinni for any more details or talk about what he is going to say at the interview. We just tell him he has an appt with the people who will help us arrest Sergio. He doesn't have to worry about what to say, it's just talking to one lady. They have special interview techniques they use to get accurate deposition from the kid to press charges." We followed these instructions.

On Thursday, December 16, I texted Felipe, "Let's be crazy and adopt a pet this weekend!" I'm glad we did not follow through on getting a dog that weekend. I was persistent in that we needed a therapy dog. And Felipe was like chill the fuck out on pets, please. Reilly also had a rational reaction to my immediate trauma response of needing to adopt a pet. She said, "It could be a nice distraction, or it could be overwhelming."

Trinny and Carmen were already talking about moving and listing the property for sale. I told them they could come to my house whenever, if they felt like they had to get away from 32 Arthur Street. Carmen told Trinny she was so embarrassed and said she couldn't face me. I responded with, "It's awful. I don't hold anything against your mom." Trinny also told her it wasn't her fault. We talked about how manipulative Sergio was. I asked about D'Aven. He had just shared his story about what happened to him. I suggested he file a report so there would be multiple charges.

Trinny also talked to me about telling Trevor. She said she had a feeling it happened to Trevor because it would explain a lot about his behavior and addiction. Neither one of us knew when Sergio would be arrested, but we were both hoping it would happen soon. At this point in time, we thought Sergio would be arrested once he was charged with his crimes. Trinny told me, "I don't know what to think or how to act at this point."

I reminded her, "He is a monster. He's not your nephew anymore. Your nephew died with this."

On Friday, December 17, I started planning our family's healing moon ceremony. It was scheduled for Saturday with Trinny and family. Trinny and I also made a plan about how to talk to Trevor.

I spoke to Dr. Kia, Vinni's pediatrician. She is amazing. Not just a doctor, but a trustworthy friend and someone I genuinely love as a person. I am so glad we switched to her when we did.

Trinny woke up that morning having an anxiety attack. All she could think about was what would happen when shit went down—when the Delgados found out we told the police about Sergio.

I told Trinny to come over around 5:00 p.m. Saturday and said there would be bracelet making, spell jars, and ice cream sundaes at the moon ceremony. She said, "That will be really nice. I'm so sorry, Erin."

I responded with, "I'm so sorry too, Trinny. This monster violated our babies. We have each other, though, and we will be OK in the end. He will not."

"Yeah. It's really hard to comprehend, though. Why? Why did he do this to us?"

"Only sick fucks understand why they commit this crime. Sergio is one of them. Tonito is dead—he was a fraud this whole time. I know I come off as insensitive sometimes, and I hope I don't upset you. Felipe is the more emotional one. I can't just cry and be a puddle of mush. My way of dealing with this was filing reports, researching shit, and completing tasks."

Saturday, December 18, I skipped the dentist. I never did go back to the dentist. I also texted Felipe, "I'm only gonna deliver one box of cookies today. I just don't have the strength to do more."

It was the night of the moon ceremony, and the moon was in Gemini—the perfect time to release pain and start healing. Of course, Illianna asked to bring her bestie, Lyanny. She is like part of the family.

Sunday, December 19, I asked Trinny if I could reach out to Trevor, and she said yes. I texted him, "Hi Trevor! It's Titi Erin. We missed you Saturday. I know you had a show and couldn't make it. Could we talk sometime this week? There is something really bad happening to my family. I talked to your mom and siblings about it, and I want to tell you what's going on. I love you. Please let me know if you can stop by."

I never did get a chance to connect with Trevor during the interim period to tell him. He found out after the Delgados found out.

On Monday, December 20, Vinni pulled that worksheet from health class out of his bag. My kids explained they only have health class for half the year, technology class the rest of the year. I texted Felipe, "I think learning about consent and the other stuff in health class helped him connect the dots that this is not normal and I need to stop it." I also told Felipe I gave up on delivering the cookies and was eating them.

On that same day, December 20, we received a Christmas card from Becca and Sergio. I threw it in the fireplace without opening it. We did not even want to see their faces. Felipe texted me saying, "I feel bad for her. She has no clue." Every point of contact from the Delgados during this time was a major anxiety trigger.

This was the day I called my doctor's office, asking for a therapist.

On Tuesday, December 21, I heard from the pediatrician's office that they had a trauma therapist that could take Vinni on as a patient. I also remember stopping at Ollie's on Grafton Street after dropping Luna off with my mom. As I was shopping the aisles with my cart, I instantly regretted shopping on this side of Worcester, in close proximity to 32 Arthur Street. I could not play it cool if I saw a Delgado. From that day forward, I've scanned every crowd that is before me, searching and bracing myself for any Delgado sightings.

This was also the night of Jess's dad's wake.

On Wednesday, December 22, D'Aven asked if he and Illianna could come over, to which I responded with of course, see you soon. There was a huge flock of ravens flying in and above and around our yard that day—like hundreds. D'Aven talked about his trauma, and he shared some stories about Nana and her acting performances. Carmen had the most pressure on her to be normal around the Delgados because she was very close to Ofelia and saw her more often than everyone else.

I talked to Trinny that morning. We were both worried about the SANE interviews scheduled for the next day. We didn't know what to expect or how things would unfold from there. We were also really scared of Sergio and how he would react to the accusations.

My pediatrician expressed much concern about there being multiple victims, and the fact that Sergio had access to twelve guns. She said she thought things might proceed very quickly because clearly, there is eminent danger. She suggested looking into getting a hotel, just in case.

Gloria texted me on this day asking if we were coming over for Christmas Eve. I didn't respond to her until the next day. I couldn't.

Thursday, December 23, was Illianna and Vinni's SANE interviews.

A giant hawk was at my bird feeder when we got home from the interview. It also perched in our tree for a while, looking for rodents below.

Trinny was not the first person of contact with Illianna's case. It was Illianna's BFF, Lyanny. After Illianna had her SANE interview, Trinny was told that Illianna's charges, if they moved forward, would be child rape, but because Sergio was fourteen years old at the time, it would be juvenile charges instead of adult. Because I was the first person of contact for Vinni, I could not be told anything about Vinni's interview. And I had to be interviewed by the detective.

At 5:16 p.m. I responded to Gloria. I said, "Hi! Because of COVID-19 being crazy right now, we decided to stay home this year." I wish I could have said what I wanted to say.

On Friday, December 24, Ofelia texted me about Vinni's shoe size. She also texted Felipe the same question. I said I was going to ignore her. Felipe texted one number in response.

My Facebook memories that day had a picture of Livi, Vinni, Mia, baby Luna, and baby Je'Nise all sitting on the couch at Nana's house. The memory was from four years ago. Vinni's four-year-old little baby face. In the background was Sergio, mouth wide open, about to take a bite of food and Becca just sitting next to him, watching him. It's too bad he didn't choke on that bite of food.

Gloria invited Jayda and Aliyah to Christmas Eve at her house. Jayda is the mother of Trevor's daughter, Aliyah. Once Trinny heard Jayda was invited to hang with the Delgados on Christmas Eve, she knew she had to tell Jayda what was going on. Jayda had to know those people were not safe people. Aliyah was only two years old. Jayda and Gloria both work at the same drug rehab clinic and were friendly with each other.

Monday, December 27, Becca posted pictures of Sergio holding Gloria's brand-new baby. She was about two months old. Trinny said she cringed every time she saw Becca's car parked outside Gloria's house, where Mia and the baby live.

On Tuesday, December 28, I scheduled Vinni's first session for trauma therapy on January 13.

On Friday, December 31, Nana saw Sergio, and she had to give him a hug to appear normal.

Sunday, January 2, Gloria tagged us all in a Facebook memory. It was a picture from eight years earlier of Trevor, D'Aven, Estela, Olivia, and Gloria. Estela commented beneath saying, "Wow, have times changed. Wish it was still the same." She had no idea how different shit was or was about to become.

On Monday, January 3, both Lyanny and I had our interviews with the detective. D'Aven asked me how it went, and I said, "The detective was nice, but I still have no idea when that piece of shit gets arrested." D'Aven told me his interview was that Thursday. The detective told me to lay low while they conducted their investigation. We laid as low as possible.

Gloria texted me again on this day asking how my kids felt after getting vaccinated for COVID-19. I said they were fine. She said she was going to get Mia vaccinated. I said, good.

On Tuesday, January 4, D'Aven had a dream that everyone found out and Sergio was arrested. Ofelia was there, and she came up to him with some paperwork. He said he woke up with so much anxiety from that dream.

Gloria texted me again asking which COVID-19 vaccine did the kids get. I told her Pfizer.

Thursday, January 6, Olivia showed me a picture of Justin Bieber she drew for her friend. It looked exactly like Justin Bieber—it was incredible. I posted it on my Facebook page, and guess who fucking commented on it. Sergio wrote, "Amazing!" Several other people also commented on it. I liked every post but his. I texted Felipe the screenshot and described how angry this made me feel. Living life on the low was getting really hard. I was a mess in so many ways but had to keep a low profile around almost everyone.

Vinni had an appointment on January 10 with a doctor, and on our way home, we stopped at the Sole Proprietor. It was the fanciest restaurant Vinni had ever eaten in. He got fried clams.

Tuesday, January 11, was a very stressful, hectic day for me. I felt alone and overwhelmed. I had a meeting with Olivia's teachers about evaluating her for dyslexia. Work was busy with client calls. And I was contacting a realtor to help get the ball rolling for listing 32 Arthur Street. The doctor we met with the day before suggested I give the DA an update about Vinni's appointment, so I did. Then my victim-witness advocate called me back saying, "Don't put things like that in writing." I sobbed that day. I lashed out at Felipe. I was scared, and I felt like I was messing up because I didn't understand the system. I was trying to be thorough and strong and QUIET. I said, "The Delgados are about to find out, and God knows what happens next."

Wednesday, January 12, I made a bomb tomato soup. I roasted red peppers, tomatoes, garlic, olive oil, etc., then blended with cream. So delicious!

We had been on edge since mid-December, waiting for when the police were going to call Sergio. We knew Trinny would be the first to hear, so we devised a plan. When she had that missed call from Sergio back on January 11, we thought something was up, but he didn't leave a voicemail or text Trinny back.

On January 12, 2022, I got the call from Trinny. She said, "The eagle has landed. He went down to the police station yesterday, and Estela went with him. Then they went to Gloria's house, and I guess Sergio was puking and throwing up from crying so much. And my dad was there. At one point they dragged my mom over from next door so she could answer questions they had about what's going on."

After I got off the phone with Trinny, I called Carmen to check on her and see if she wanted me to pick her up and take her away from 32 Arthur Street. I made the same offer to Illianna so she wouldn't have to stay in that house at this elevated moment. Felipe and I decided at one point that depending on how the Delgados reacted to this news, we might just get a hotel room in some random town nearby just to not be in Worcester where they could find us.

This was the first time Carmen started to waver. I asked her if she was OK and if she wanted to come to my house, and she said no. I asked her what the Delgados said. She told me Sergio was denying the accusations and said he never did anything. There was confusion as to what happened and when. Ofelia told her it doesn't make sense. Carmen let out a "I don't know what to do. This is all so confusing."

This was my very first time getting gangsta with my mother-in-law. I told her, "Kids don't lie about being molested. You know Vinni is telling the truth, don't you? You saw when Sergio came down those stairs and into your home and asked only for Vinni, over and over again. You cannot be manipulated by Ofelia. We are going through this shit together, and we will help each other heal, but the Delgados aren't our family anymore. This is gang shit now, Carmen! You fuck with the Delgados, I don't fuck with you! I don't want it to come down to that, and I

know this is wicked hard on all of us, but do not listen to them!"
Carmen mostly cried on the other end as my fluctuations of aggression and sadness spilled out into the phone. I ended with, "I'll call you later when things are a little more settled down. I love you."

This was the day the eagle landed. We didn't know what to expect. Felipe originally planned to go to his mom's that night to meet with the realtor, but now the plan was completely changed. This was the night of the family meeting. From the family meeting, D'Aven texted me and said, "We're just digesting everything, and Ofelia is literally dying inside...I don't know if it's the empath in me, but I feel so bad. Like no one saw this coming, all from the hands of this man who chose to do all this. I keep trying to tell her he's grown and made his own choices. She's apologizing to us each, and crying so much. Never saw her like this." He also told me Estela was crying too, but she was more so consoling her mother and not so much showing sympathy toward her cousins.

On Thursday, January 13, Vinni had his first session of virtual trauma therapy. This is also allegedly the day I began criminally harassing Sergio. Although I did not have any contact with Sergio on this day, I did hear through the grapevine that Sergio told Ofelia he would take a lie detector test or be hypnotized for questioning. This is also when Ofelia became confused about what to believe. This was the exact moment when she completely disregarded everything that was said at the family meeting the night before.

We all felt so vulnerable and worried during the interim period. It was an anxiety only we could understand, and it was just the beginning.

My Vinicio

When Olivia was about six months old, I unexpectedly found myself pregnant. The second I saw the confirmation on the pregnancy test, I started sobbing. I did not want to be pregnant. I wasn't ready to be pregnant again, and I wanted more time alone with my firstborn. I didn't even tell Felipe. I just left the test on the bathroom counter, and he found it after work.

I remember him walking into the living room smiling ear to ear, asking, "You're pregnant?!?"

I burst out crying and said, "Yes." I cried because I didn't want to be pregnant, and I cried because I felt guilty about not being excited. I was so excited to find out I was pregnant with Olivia, and this pregnancy, well, this child, deserved to have that too.

After a couple weeks, the pregnancy sunk in a bit more, and my mindset became more positive. I remember thinking, "It's another girl, and she and Liv will be best friends." They would be fifteen months apart. Two under two. My mom had two kids close in age, I could do it too.

When I went for my first ultrasound, Felipe was able to meet me at the appointment. We both looked over at the screen and waited for the ultrasound tech lady to explain what we were looking at. As she started, she asked, "Have you had a lot of cramping? Or bleeding?" I said, no. I didn't notice much difference between how I felt pregnant with Olivia and this one. Then she pointed at the monitor and said, "Do you see this right here, about an inch long? Well, at seven weeks pregnant, an embryo should measure twice this size. See how there is no movement or flickering? It's not a viable pregnancy. Do you guys understand what I'm saying?"

"Yup." Loud and clear, ultrasound lady. I said, "Our baby's dead."

"I'm really sorry. I'm going to tell the doctor, and he can go over your options in more depth. You can schedule a D&C or wait and miscarry naturally. I'm really sorry for your loss." She walked out, and a few minutes later the doctor walked in. Me and Felipe were in shock. We were just told, very bluntly, that we were not going to have another baby right now.

I started crying over the loss of this baby. And I struggled with guilt, feeling like I caused it. What if my gut reaction of not wanting this baby sent a signal to the embryo telling it not to grow? I decided to miscarry naturally and not have a D&C.

I always thought that you found out you were having a miscarriage when you started bleeding profusely. That was not the case for me. I did not start bleeding or expelling the miscarriage until about ten days later. I had so much anxiety during this time, just waiting to bleed and expel my uterus.

The night it started, I had just sat down with a glass of wine. A few sips in, I noticed a cramping sensation that was becoming more and more regular, and I was spotting. It didn't amount to much, and I was tired, so I went to bed. When I woke up the next day, the labor sensations were still there, so I called in sick to work. I dropped Olivia off at Mary's house, then came back home. I remember my back hurting and feeling like I had to go to the bathroom, so I sat on the toilet. It did feel like labor, but not as strong and not nearly as painful as actual labor. I looked down into the toilet afterward and saw this little sac that looked like a small water balloon. WARNING: This part is graphic. Skip down to the next paragraph if you don't want to read. WARNING! Anyways, I had to open the sac and see what it looked like. So I did. Inside was a tubelike entity, unrecognizable. It was not a tiny humanlike, alien-looking embryo. It was a bunch of malformed cells. I flushed it all away.

I was relieved to put that miscarriage behind me. That pregnancy felt like one giant rollercoaster. In the end, I am happy that pregnancy did not thrive because if it did, I might not have my Vinicio.

We waited until Olivia was about eighteen months old to start trying for our next baby. With Olivia, I got pregnant the second I stopped birth control. This time around, I didn't get pregnant the first month. Oh well, maybe next month. Nothing. The months came and went. I started to worry that maybe we wouldn't have any more babies.

Felipe and I talked about it, and we decided not to stress about trying, and whenever the timing was right, I would get pregnant. If we only got one baby, we only got one baby, and we would be fine. I decided to quit my job at the accounting firm, and I opened a store called Wild Orchid Baby. It was a place where moms could shop for organic baby products and also socialize at baby & me yoga, breastfeeding class, mom groups, etc. Olivia liked working at my store with me. It started as an online shop, but I signed a lease for a brick and mortar that November.

Right after Thanksgiving, I noticed my period was a few days late. I took a pregnancy test the day after attending a bachelorette party. I was pregnant. I was ecstatic! I called the doctor, and they scheduled my first ultrasound. When I went for my appointment, my excitement turned to anxiety. Felipe was not able to meet me at the appointment, so I was going alone. I was worried it might not be a viable pregnancy again.

I went to the room and got undressed and lay on the table. The ultrasound lady walked in. It was the exact same ultrasound lady who had told me my baby was dead the last time I was pregnant. Just the sight of her retraumatized me. She looked at my chart and bluntly said, "Ummm...based on the date of your last missed period, you're only five weeks, four days. I won't even be able to see anything until at least six weeks. They shouldn't have scheduled your appointment so soon. I'm sorry, but you're going to have to come back in a week or two."

"OK." I was happy to get dressed and leave that place. I went back to my appointment a week or two later. I was still anxious about the appointment, but once the ultrasound lady walked in and it wasn't that lady from before, I felt calm, and peace come over me. She pointed out my embryo, which was measuring perfectly normal for seven weeks, and we heard the heartbeat on the Doppler. A few months later, on Felipe's birthday, March 12, we found out this baby was a boy. We immediately settled on the name Vinicio but refused to tell anyone. We did not want nobody's fucking opinions, so we decided to tell nobody what we were naming him.

Just before I got pregnant with Vinni, I agreed to be the maid of honor in Reilly's wedding. Her wedding was August 10. And my due date with Vinni was August 9—no big deal, it will all be fine. I explained to Reilly that there was a definite possibility that I would be in labor, or still be pregnant or extremely postpartum at her wedding. I would not be a hot, unswollen bridesmaid; I might not even make it to the actual wedding day. I told her if she wanted to choose someone else now that I have discovered I'm pregnant, she should. But she said, "No way. I want you."

So, I canceled my normal-sized bridesmaid dress and ordered a maternity style big enough to house a nine monther. I figured if I had the baby beforehand, we could just carve out some excess fabric and make the dress look normal. It was all I could do, really.

On July 27, 2013, I woke up and felt a trickle of fluid come out of me. I went to the bathroom and took a shower. While I was doing my hair, I started feeling regular cramps. I put two and two together and realized I was probably in labor. This was a great day to have the baby! Reilly's wedding was two weeks away. I told Felipe I was fine to go work at my store for a few hours. I arranged for my friend Stacey to come work for me that afternoon, so I told him to pick me up around then. In the meantime, the hospital was just up the street. I could figure out a way to get there sooner if need be.

By the time Felipe picked me up, I was having a lot of back labor. We headed up to the hospital. I planned to have a natural birth, like I did with Olivia. Upon arriving, the doctor suggested Pitocin, which freaked me out. My mom said she had Pitocin in labor with me and it sucked ass. She said if you can avoid it, do it. I said no, I didn't want it. Hours later, I was still having horrible back labor. I was exhausted, in pain. I got the drugs—all the drugs. First it was a shot of something for pain, then Pitocin. Then the full-on epidural.

Baby's heart rate kept dropping. I had to keep going on my hands and knees. My fluid was all gone at this point. I had a tube pumping fluid into my uterus. I felt like a giant bag of shit. I remember finally getting comfortable and resting for a bit. I had already been at the hospital for eighteen hours. I saw so many nurse shift changes. My epidural was wearing off, and I could feel my baby slipping down my birth canal. Each contraction brought him a tiny bit closer earthside.

I said to myself, "I'm not fucking telling anybody. I just want to lie here, and the baby can slide right out." So that's what I did. Inevitably though, minutes later, the nurse was back in asking to check me again. I told her I was ready and could feel the baby coming.

The hospital team gathered around and said, "OK, you can start pushing, but if his heart rate drops again, we need to do an emergency C-section."

I said, "No. I will push him right out. Like so fast. I don't need a C-section." I pushed once, his heart rate dropped, and the monitors started beeping like crazy. Everyone rushed me to the OR. I was placed on a different table. Felipe got geared up head to toe in his operation suit. I was given a big dose of medicine that made me very numb. I said again, "I will push him out. I don't need a C-section."

The doctors said, "OK, but you need to push him out right now!"

I mustered all the strength I had, even though I was numb from the waist down from the fresh dose of C-section drugs. I pushed as hard as I could, and Vinni was born in seconds. He was finally here, and he was perfect. But I quickly realized my sweet little guy had been through the ringer too, with that traumatic birth. He had a small mark on his forehead from the amniotic fluid tube. Also, he had the head monitor screwed into the top of his skull. It broke my heart knowing my tiny newborn had already experienced so much birth trauma compared to my first child, but here he was. My perfect little Vinicio. He had my boobs now, and that's basically all he needed to keep him happy at this point. He nursed and spit up constantly. Nurse, spit up, nurse some more, spit up.

Vinni was hands down the most beautiful baby I have ever seen. Listen, my girls were absolutely gorgeous babies, and they are gorgeous to this day, but Vinni? Vinni just had this absolute stunning look to him. Everyone noticed it. No matter what I dressed him in, everybody would say, "She is absolutely gorgeous! Her eyes, her lashes, her hair, her smile!" Even if he was dressed in boy clothes, Vinni was just too pretty.

He had long hair as a baby too. I think he was around six months old when Shayne cut his hair for the first time. That's when we noticed his double swirl in the back of his head. Most people have one swirl that their hair grows from. He is unique for having two.

Vinni never wanted to sleep in his crib. He was very attached to me. The rare occasion we did get him to sleep in the crib, he would climb out. I took a video once of baby Vinni showing me how he climbs out. He's less than two years old in it, and it's fucking adorable and hilarious. I also remember Felipe putting him down for a nap when he was two. It was the day of his birthday party. When we went to get him after he woke up, he had climbed out of the bed and covered his face and hair with diaper cream. Like what the fuck, bro? He got a toy vacuum from Stacey at that birthday, and it was his favorite thing ever. For some reason, he was fascinated by vacuums as a toddler.

He has always been the best eater of my kids, always preferring the adult food over chicken nuggets and pizza. When he was four years old, he fell off the monkey bars and broke his elbow. He needed surgery to pin the bone in place. When he woke up, the nurse brought in a tray of food. Hospital food—Jell-O, soup, toast, applesauce. I said, "Hey Vinni, how are you doing? Do you want to try to eat something?"

He groggily responded saying, "I'll have the salmon." I laughed and said his options were more like Jell-O or applesauce right now. I told him I'd make salmon later once we were home from the hospital. He had a roommate in that hospital room—a toddler who cried almost the whole time we were there. He was chronically ill, so he and his mother spent a lot of time at the hospital. I felt really bad for them and how hard it must be having a sick child. Vinni breaking his arm was scary enough, but at least he would recover and go back to normal.

Vinni is now nine years old. He loves the movie *Mean Girls*. He loves archery and making bow and arrows. He loves clay and sculpting. He loves obsidian and can make all kinds of stuff from it. He is very mature for his age and is not afraid to speak his mind. He is loving and affectionate, but not afraid to set boundaries.

Vinni is the best son in the whole world. We need to help take the bricks off his back. Too many have been stacked on him. He explained to me one time that when he feels really happy and free, it feels like a brick comes off. The weight is heavy, and I'm not sure how many are left, but I will never stop trying to help you, my Vinicio.

Fucking Pervert

"Babe, maybe we should call a lawyer." My husband suggested contacting a defense attorney as soon as we received the criminal harassment paperwork. He wasn't the only one, either.

"You should call a lawyer." —my mom.

"Have you talked to an attorney?" —my friends.

"Definitely call a lawyer." —my therapist.

"You're calling an attorney, right?" —pretty much every person I've shared my criminal harassment story with has brought up seeking legal advice.

"But why do I need a lawyer?" I respond passionately. "I didn't do anything wrong! The system is fucked up, and I shouldn't have to pay a lawyer just because Sergio is retaliating!" Everyone agrees with these facts; however, they all still strongly encourage me to at least speak to an attorney before December 7.

I don't know the right lawyers, but a friend of mine does. I texted her saying, "Are any of your siblings defense attorneys?

Asking for a friend..." She responded back, inquiring if it was DUI or worse. She also said she really did hope this was for a friend. I told her, "It's for a friend named Sweet Polly. And it's criminal harassment, up to two and a half years, one-thousand-dollar fine." Sweet Polly Purebred was one of my nicknames at city hall. I also went by RBF, which stands for Resting Bitch Face.

"Jesus." she texted back and, "I'm on it." She didn't ask any further questions and sent a referral that same day. A couple days later, I still hadn't called the attorney, but I decided to stop by city hall and give her an explanation about why I needed an attorney.

The treasury office looked really nice and professional when I walked through it. The carpet was new, and there were plexiglass dividers and new cubicles. I sat down in my friend's cube, on the chair with her French fry pillow.

She cut right to the chase. "So, what's going on? Because I can tell by your face this is some shit you're dealing with."

"Yeah. My family's been dealing with something really bad for the past year, and it's the reason why I need to talk to a lawyer."

"Please don't tell me something happened to your daughter."

"It's my son." I didn't have to tell her any more details; she just instinctively knew what happened. She said she had a friend who dealt with a similar situation with her daughter, and that the perpetrator was a family member. I told her that's what we were dealing with as well. When she asked me what I actually did to incur the charges, I said, "I ran my mouth on social media. I announced his arraignment and said he was an unsafe person, not allowed to be around kids."

She was heartbroken. Working at city hall with me, she saw my kids on snow days and any other time I had day care issues and had to bring them to work. One time she took Olivia to Coney Island for lunch while I was in a budget meeting.

She gave me a big hug and said, "I know why you did what you did, and you're not wrong. But you need to at least call the lawyer because you cannot say the wrong thing at court. And we all know how likely you are to fly right off the fucking handle! Rightfully so, but still." I promised her I would at least call the attorney.

Two days later it was Sunday, November 20, and it was a frigid day in Worcester. Vinni had a friend sleep over the night before, and thankfully, they had just gotten picked up. Felipe had also just left to go to the grocery store. I was hanging out with Luna in the living room when the doorbell rang. Luna ran to look out the window and announced, "Mom, the police is here!"

I answered the front door braless, in my pajamas and bathrobe—my usual Sunday morning attire. Officer Rivera remained on my front steps as he introduced himself and requested to speak to Erin Arvizu. I had a feeling the police were there for me. He said, "I am here to serve you with a restraining order from Ofelia..." As he looked down at the paperwork to confirm the last name, I finished his sentence for him. Ofelia Delgado. I knew who would have filed the order.

I asked if I needed to come outside, and he said that wasn't necessary; he was just going to hand me the paperwork. He also said, "You should call the courthouse on Monday. Do you see this section here that says, 'Modification Date November 18'? Well, that could mean that it's not active, so you should call to see if the hearing is actually scheduled. What is your relationship to Ofelia?"

"She is my husband's sister. We have been in our situation for about a year now. Her son, Sergio, sexually abused my son, and we are prosecuting him. I have not seen Ofelia at all, aside from when we are at court. I have not spoken to her in almost a year. She is retaliating against us. I have criminal harassment charges that were filed against me from Sergio too."

"You should definitely call the courthouse Monday to see where the order stands." While he served the order to me, our neighbor walked by with the dog that lives next door.

Now I have a restraining order and criminal harassment charges filed against me. It's as if the Delgados are filing whatever they can against me to harass me.

Mia turned seven years old last weekend. Gloria threw her a big birthday party at a hall, just like she always does. I bet there were fancy cookies, matching T-shirts, and maybe even a piñata or a candy bar. I also know that Sergio was at Mia's birthday party, along with Becca, Becca's mother, Felipe Sr., Doña Ofelia, and the rest of the enablers. The photo I saw, through the social media grapevine, shows Sergio wearing a face mask, and he's talking to his father, Tony. Sergio is the only person wearing a mask at the party, or so it appears in this picture.

He is hiding his face. He does this at court as well. No one else wears a mask but him. I hope Rotten Fruit is the reason he feels uncomfortable being at Mia's birthday party. I hope there were people at this party that heard he is unsafe, and I hope they heard it from Rotten Fruit. I hope there were people that decided not to attend the party because of what they saw on Rotten Fruit. Mia has no voice right now. She is surrounded by enablers. They invited this fucking pervert to her birthday party.

Before I called the attorney's office, I walked down to the courthouse to get the affidavits for my crimes. I walked over to the annex section and asked the woman if I could have the affidavit pertaining to my restraining order. She asked, "Were you the complainant?" I explained that no, I was the person the restraining order was filed against. I said I was served yesterday morning by the police. She asked for my ID and printed the affidavit.

I thanked her, and then I asked, "Are you able to look up criminal charges as well? I have a criminal harassment charge against me, and would like the affidavit for that too, if that's possible." She printed out that one too and handed it to me. "Thank you very much!" I walked back up to my office.

Ofelia's affidavit for the restraining order says:

Erin made a Facebook and posted a photo of me and she asked a question on the post and someone commented "I would have murder thoughts" and she liked it. That put me in fear for my life. I know she is capable of harming me or getting someone else to do it. In September she made Tik Toks with my photos and stated some remarks that is Defamation of my character of a serious matter. She has also sent messages in messenger to close friends of mine to lie about me. They have reached out to me in disbelief. Someone close to me has expressed their concerns about my safety due to her behavior and stuff that was said about me. Example she expressed anger towards me with them. I'm also in fear for my granddaughter. She has posted picture of her as well and she is 7 years old, without permission on Tik Toks and Facebook the one she made and her personal one. My son also has a pending harassment/criminal case against Erin Arvizu for this similar reasons. Because of Erin's actions I'm feeling distressed, I can't sleep. I don't feel safe and I fear for my life and safety because I know she is capable of harming me herself or sending someone else to harm me. This are the reasons I'm requesting a restraining order.

On my restraining order paperwork, the first box is checked off, which says, "This order was issued without advance notice because the Court determined that there is a substantial likelihood of immediate danger of abuse." This box was not checked off on the restraining order Felipe filed against Sergio.

Sergio's affidavit for the criminal harassment charge says:

On January 13th 2022 Erin messaged my wife causing alarm and distress after she filed for a restraining order against me and we were ordered to not have contact with her or them with us. She also went on to react to my wife's social media even though at this point my wife had unfriended her (Erin time and time again went out of her way to harass/stalk). Also on the same day she directly messaged my sister calling me a "fucking monster." The third event causing me mental distress and alarm was on the same day as well when she posted my photo on social media and labelled me "Rotten Fruit." Other events have occurred, see pictures and evidence. The most recent alarming event that has caused me distress due to fear of retaliation was Oct 19th Erin Arvizu shared the page I believe she created on her social media with my picture, name, family and where I reside.

He forgot to mention his arraignment and the terms of his probation—those were also included on the October 19 Facebook post. On this official court document, his printed name reads, "Sergio Antonio Felipe Delgado." Like what the fuck is this dude's actual, real name?

Well, I forwarded the paperwork to the law office I was referred to, and I am meeting with the attorney tomorrow afternoon. In the meantime, I'm writing this chapter to help me process, reconcile, and move forward with my life. The chapters kind of write themselves at this point. I do yearn for closure, though. I want to end this book. And I want court to end for good.

Let's break these official court documents down. Ofelia's affidavit is up first. The first lie she tells is actually the opening line of her story. She says, "Erin made a Facebook and posted a photo of me and she asked a question on the post and some one commented 'I would have murder thoughts' and she liked it." The post she is referencing, where I ask the question, "How would you react if a child reported sexual abuse?"—this post only contains a picture of a children's book and Sergio's face, not Ofelia's photo at all. Next, the commenter wrote, "I would have murder dreams," not thoughts. Beneath this comment, I wrote how Jessie, the author of the children's book, tells kids to keep telling adults until someone believes them.

Further down Ofelia writes, "In September she made Tik Toks with my photos and stated some remarks that is defamation of my character of a serious matter." First of all, I used Becca's photos, not Ofelia's. Secondly, I called her out for being an enabler because she allowed her son to sexually abuse four children in her home. Sergio had access to his bedroom at his mom's house even after he had moved out and was married. For her to prove defamation, she would have to prove the statements I made are false.

The next line is another flat-out lie. She says, "She has also sent messages in messenger to close friends of mine to lie about me. They have reached out to me in disbelief." I don't message any of Ofelia's friends. I have a strict arm's-length-distance rule—aka, you fuck with the Delgados, I don't fuck with you.

This one is the worst part in the whole entire document though. Where she says, "I'm also in fear for my granddaughter. She has posted picture of her as well and she is 7 years old, without permission on Tik Toks and Facebook the one she made and her personal one." When Felipe asked Ofelia to talk to Mia, back at the family meeting, she completely blew it off. Then she confirmed that fucking pervert was at Mia's house. We all have reason to believe Mia was being groomed and/or molested alongside Vinni. Ofelia doesn't protect her granddaughter from that fucking pervert but will use her as a pawn to file a restraining order.

I only have one thing I want to say about Sergio's affidavit, even though it also contains multiple lies like his mother's. It's in reference to the part where he says, "she directly messaged my sister calling me a 'fucking monster.'" I most certainly did not. When I texted Gloria that day, I called him a fucking pervert. By changing my word to monster, he removes my intention.

Felipe and I met with the attorney, and we liked him a lot. He had an excellent understanding of our situation from the timeline I sent, and he asked questions to fill in the information he needed more clarification on. He said our case was bizarre, and it pissed him off that I would even need to consider hiring a lawyer. He gave us some great advice and called the DA. He said as long as I felt confident prevailing at both hearings on my own, I should do that, but of course he was available to represent me for $5,000.

I decided to face the fucking pervert and the restraining order hoe at court, alone, without legal representation.

Restraining Order Hoe

The night before my restraining order hearing, I went to bed early. I woke up around 4:00 a.m. because I got my period. Seeing my period show up in time for court let me know my body felt safe. When Vinni first disclosed his truth to me last year, my period was about ten days late due to stress. My body was in fight-or-flight mode and was not ready to begin another cycle until we felt safe.

We got to court early that morning—around 8:30 a.m. I told Felipe we had to get a parking spot on Main Street because I was wearing my red heels and didn't want to walk all the way from the garage. At some point, months ago, on a day when I felt angry and everything felt impossible, I printed out some Sergio flyers. They contain his picture, age, arraignment, etc. I never did anything with these flyers until the day of my restraining order hearing. I clipped one to the outside of my folder, making Sergio's face visible for all to see at the courthouse. We entered the front doors and went through security without issue. We were told my hearing would be in courtroom 24. We went upstairs to the fourth floor and waited for court to open.

It was about 8:50 a.m. Illianna was pacing around, looking to see when the Delgados would arrive. My support team consisted of Felipe and Illianna by my side that day. Someone who worked at the courthouse announced to everyone that restraining orders were moved downstairs to courtroom 16, so we walked one flight down the stairs and sat on the left side of the courtroom.

Eventually, the circus trickled in. Ofelia, Felipe Sr., and Maria were there. Later on, Ofelia's friend Shauna arrived. Shauna once sent me a message on Rotten Fruit saying, "Wow you're a committed hater. You got time huh." I blasted her message and my response on the actual Facebook wall for all to see. My response to her was, "Committed to protecting children. I hope you do the same. Child molestation causes a lifetime of trauma."

Maybe this was the message Ofelia was referencing in her affidavit? It would explain Shauna's appearance at court. Welcome to the circus, Shauna—clowns to the right. We sat in the courtroom for a long time before my case was called. At first, I felt a lot of anxiety each time a case wrapped up because I was so nervous my case would be next. After an hour and a half, however, I was actually hoping to be called next, just to get the hearing over with. It's long and boring sitting in a courtroom waiting for your case. It was so long and boring that Maria actually fell asleep.

I heard a loud growling noise at one point. I was thinking, what the fuck was that? That is one super powerful stomach growl, if that's what that bear noise was. It legit sounded like a bear snuck into the courtroom and growled, but it was just Maria snoring. She passed out and snored really loudly, twice. Felipe Sr. got up out of his seat and went over to her. He was nudging her and talking in her ear to wake her up. During this time, the judge had called the next case forward, and the plaintiff couldn't get out of the row because Senior was blocking her way, trying to wake up sleepy clown. A court officer asked the circus to look alive and clear the aisle.

They finally called my case, and I'm glad Maria was awake to witness the main event. Ofelia and I each walked up to our opposing podiums. I set my paperwork down in three piles. The judge took a few minutes to read through Ofelia's affidavit and whatever other evidence she submitted. I felt nervous but relieved to be getting it over with. The judge turned to me and said, "Would you like to extend the restraining order?"

Caught off guard, I replied, "Uhh, I'm the person the restraining order is against." I forgot to address the judge as Your Honor throughout the entire hearing—we all make mistakes. But I would like to address this white privilege moment. Being mistaken for the plaintiff more than once speaks volumes about what the courtroom looks like in reality. When you are sitting down in the audience and viewing the proceedings, it appears the court system is run by mostly white people, and the people catching these cases are mostly people of color. There are white people in trouble and people of color working for the system—I'm not saying there are not—I am saying exactly what I see in the actual courtroom I sit in each time I am there. Me, a professional, educated, small-stature white woman—I had to remind the system twice that I was the defendant because I do not look anything like the majority of the defendants I see at court.

What is the opposite of white privilege? For Felipe, it's Hispanic oppression. People assume I am good and assume Felipe is not good. When I was naked, draped only in a johnny, while in labor with Olivia, several hospital staff asked me if Felipe was a friend of the family. I had to explain, more than once, that Felipe is my husband/father of my child. In September when we checked in with the DA's office for Sergio's hearing, in the courthouse victim chambers, after giving my name, Erin Arvizu, and the name of the defendant in our case, the guy at the counter asked if Felipe was Sergio Delgado. Ummm no, the defendant is absolutely NOT standing next to me, the mother of the child victim. Once again, everyone, Felipe is my husband and the father of my child.

Today, I am the defendant. Now, back to the hearing.

The judge noticed his slipup and said, "Oh right. I apologize. Do you oppose the restraining order?"

I said, "Yes."

The judge turned to Ofelia and explained the law. He said, "For me to extend this restraining order, I must hear evidence that there was harm, or attempt to cause harm, or events that caused you to feel eminent fear. What is the basis to support your claims?" Then the train wreck started.

Ofelia rambled on and on about how I created a TikTok account and a Facebook account and I posted her information, where she lives, and that I called them enablers and posted pictures of her granddaughter.

The judge kept asking her to be specific. What exactly did the defendant say or do? Ofelia said I keep posting about an issue and that a close family member has expressed concern about her safety. She said her mother thinks me and Felipe won't be happy until something is done to her son. The judge asked her specifically what I said to her mother. Ofelia said I call her mother all the time, yelling at her. The judge said, "So your mother expressed her opinion to you about your safety?" Ofelia said yes and the judge said well, that is irrelevant.

Ofelia said I keep posting about an issue. The judge asked what the issue was. She said it was a case that had to do with her son. The judge asked what kind of case her son had. She said I was calling her an enabler and saying her son is a bad person. She said she thinks we condone what he's been accused of. The judge asked her what her son has been accused of, and she finally said the word, "Molestation."

Next, the judge asked her to elaborate on the murder comment. She talked in circles again, about how I have criminal charges filed against me, how she fears for her granddaughter, how I'm still posting all of her information on social media. Then...OK, this is one of my favorite parts. Ofelia says, "The last time Erin posted on Facebook was on November 29, and she used my name. Erin said, 'His mother, Ofelia, is going nuts with restraining orders.'" I could not contain my reaction when I heard this one. Like, why the fuck have we all been gathered here for two hours, Ofelia? Because you're a RESTRAINING ORDER HOE! I wish I would have said that on my Facebook just to hear her call herself a restraining order hoe in court.

It felt like I stood there for ten minutes listening to her spew lies and bullshit. Finally, it was my turn to speak. I was blunt, per usual, but also truthful and powerful. I read the first line in her affidavit and held up the printouts of what I posted on Facebook. I read my question aloud and the comments to show there was nothing threatening about my post. Then I shared the crux of the matter. I said Sergio sexually abused my son for four years when he was between the ages of four and eight. I said three more cousins have also come forward saying Sergio sexually assaulted them. I said we pressed charges, and he has court next week. I said it was the final compliance hearing when the trial date would be set. My response was very short, especially in comparison to the train wreck.

The judge then reiterated the law to Ofelia, saying in order to extend the restraining order, he must hear evidence of harm, attempt to cause harm or fear, blah blah blah. Then he said based on what he had read, and the testimony heard, he was terminating the restraining order!

I said thank you to the judge. Then I turned to the trial court officer and asked if I had to wait for Ofelia to exit the courtroom first. He said nope, you're free to go. I strategically placed my folder in my arms so the whole right side of the courtroom caught a glimpse of Sergio Delgado's face—especially the circus clowns. I grabbed my coat and bag from Illianna and Felipe, and we left the courtroom. The restraining order hoe chased after me, videoing our exit. She is formulating her next move. She probably has footage of the flyer clipped to my folder and Felipe and I high-fiving as we entered the lobby. I emailed the DA's office with my restraining order results and evidence I presented. I asked the state of Massachusetts to charge that restraining order hoe with perjury. This is blatant abuse of the judicial system.

Felipe's Boyfriend

The day after my criminal harassment hearing, I still felt freshly traumatized. I had a hair appointment at 10:00 a.m. that day, and at first I wasn't sure if that would be a good thing or bad thing because I am one of those people that does crazy things to their hair in moments of stress. I texted Tanya, my longtime hairdresser. We've been together even longer than me and Felipe.

I said, "Tanya...what should we do to my hair today? Mentally, I am in a bad place, so I need to do something crazy. But with no bangs." I'm not dumb. I wouldn't make that mistake again, getting bangs. She asked if everything was OK and said she would think about some options. I told her, "No. I had court yesterday. It's a long story."

She said, "OK. I think you should touch up your front for sure. Maybe some crazy color in the back? It will only take on the lighter pieces." I said OK. She knows what she's doing, and I trust her. Then I texted her my preappointment trauma dump overview, so she could really understand how close I was to having a Britney Spears trauma moment.

As we were backing out of the driveway to go to school, I told my kids I might do something crazy with my hair because I was feeling stressed out. One of them asked what had happened to Britney Spears the time she shaved her head. I said, "Well, kids, Britney Spears became the princess of pop at a very early age, like when she was still a teenager. She had a lot of pressure on her when she was very young. Then she got married and had two kids close together, which is extremely stressful for a new mom. And her relationship with K-Fed fell apart. And her parents were abusive and made her work to support them. I mean, I understand why she felt traumatized and why she took it out on her hair."

"But why did she shave her head?" they asked.

"Britney asked the hair stylist to shave her head, but the stylist refused. Then Britney saw the clippers on the counter and grabbed them. I think she shaved her head to liberate herself—cut off the dead weight and shock the world. I'm not gonna do that today, kids. Don't worry. And like the hairdresser Britney saw, Tanya would never shave my head either, even if I asked her to."

As soon as I sat in Tanya's chair, I told her she had to fix my whole life through my hair. She said, "I'm gonna take care of you. We're going to add blond to the front, like we've been doing, and I'll add some highlights throughout. Then I'll do a darker toner to give it an overall darker look—"

"Like my soul," I interrupted.

She giggled and continued with her plan. "Your highlights will look more caramel colored and get lighter as it fades. Lengthwise, I'm thinking a couple inches shorter, so it sits right at your shoulders. It will rejuvenate your curls. You will have a brand-new look but can still go back to the bright blond highlights when you're ready."

To be honest, writing this chapter has me tearing up thinking about how loved and supported Tanya made me feel that day. She really did lift me up in so many ways just by listening to me vent about my fucked-up life and doing what she does best—my hair. I wish Britney would have sat in Tanya's chair that day she shaved her head. I think if she had experienced true friendship and hair therapy from someone like Tanya, it might have changed her life, or at least lifted her up in that moment, when she needed it most.

A few days before my criminal harassment hearing, I called the courthouse to see if I was supposed to check in at the annex like I did for my restraining order. The woman told me that magistrate hearings were done online, through Zoom. I asked her for the meeting ID and password, and she provided it. This was annoying, trying to coordinate where to do my Zoom hearing and then be at Sergio's hearing as well, since they were both scheduled on the same day.

The day before my hearing, my victim-witness advocate called me. She said I could do the Zoom hearing from the courthouse, but that the Wi-Fi was unreliable and there were no private rooms available. I told her I was probably going to do the hearing from my office, then head to the courthouse afterward. I said I wanted to be present at Sergio's hearing, if possible. She explained that since court opened at 9:00 a.m., she didn't know when Sergio's hearing would be called. She said Sergio had to be present at my hearing, but that his attorney could represent him at his criminal hearing, so if they happened to be at the same time, I would miss Sergio's criminal hearing. I understood. I didn't think this was fair, but there wasn't anything I could do about it.

The morning of my hearing, we stopped at Inhouse, my favorite coffee shop, for smoothies and headed to my office. My friend Stacey met us there for moral support. My victim-witness advocate called me while we were driving, and she said, "Sergio's attorney has another case to tend to this morning, so Sergio's criminal hearing will most likely be later than yours." I thanked her and thought, well that worked out, I guess. I was so wrong.

I set up my laptop on my gray desk where I usually meet with my clients. Felipe and Stacey sat in my two client chairs. It looked like I was in a meeting, but in reality I was waiting in a Zoom room for my magistrate hearing to start. It finally did, around 9:45 a.m. Sergio and his attorney popped up on one screen, and the clerk was on the other. Sergio's attorney, let's just refer to him as Slimelick. We all know exactly what case he had to attend to this morning—mine.

Right off the bat, Slimelick was scolded by the clerk for not shutting the fuck up. The clerk was trying to swear in the fucking pervert and myself, and Slimelick kept speaking out of turn. The clerk told him to cut it out. Then Sergio and his attorney were having technical difficulties and kept breaking up. They had to call in on speakerphone and were not on camera for the remainder of the hearing. Slimelick then announced, "The defendant's husband's boyfriend was harassing my client just this morning!"

I stared in silence at the screen, on the edge of my seat, dying to know exactly who Felipe's boyfriend was. Slimelick eventually corrected himself and said, "I mean best friend. The defendant's husband's best friend. Why was Eric at the courthouse today?"

The clerk looked at me to answer. I said, "I'm not at the courthouse right now, so I don't know exactly who is there. He probably went to support our family members." I can't remember if it was the clerk who asked me which family members were at the courthouse or Slimelick, but I said, "I know my sister-in-law Trinny is there with her family."

Slimelick then declared, "We wanted to file witness intimidation against her, but we couldn't because Sergio's the defendant in that other case." The clerk asked what that other case was. Slimelick replied, "Indecent assault and battery."

"On a minor under fourteen," I chimed in. The clerk became aware of our actual situation now. The clerk asked who the victim in that case was, and I said, "My son."

Sergio and Slimelick carried on about my Facebook and TikTok posts. Sergio said, "I'm so stressed because of her. Sometimes my dog barks in the middle of the night, and it scares me. I don't know who might be outside in the bushes. I fear for my life! She posted where I live, my family, everything!" Slimelick elaborated, saying they had to do something, or she wasn't going to stop posting on her account and the Rotten Fruit one. The clerk asked if they had proof I was behind Rotten Fruit account, and they said yes.

Eventually, the clerk asked me if I would like to speak. I said yes. I referred to the affidavit Sergio submitted and read aloud the first two examples, which were the message to Becca and the text to Gloria. Slimelick interrupted me and said, "That's old stuff. We want to talk about the Facebook stuff." The clerk reminded him they were listed on the affidavit, which was just filed in late October.

When I got the floor back, I started talking about what was happening on January 13, the alleged date the harassment began. I talked about how Sergio had just been questioned by police around that time for sexually assaulting three of his cousins. I said he told the police he wasn't sure what he was going to tell his wife, so we didn't think he was telling her the truth about anything that was going on. I said he admitted to assaulting

D'Aven and told police his father walked in on it. I said he told the detective that Vinni and Illianna were the inappropriate ones, not him. Slimelick interrupted me, and the clerk joined in, both agreeing that I wasn't allowed to talk about Sergio's other case.

How come Slimelick can talk about Felipe's boyfriend and mention an incident that happened that very morning without my knowledge, but I can't talk about the actual reason why we are gathered here today? The reason is speaking about Sergio's other case.

Then I said, "We filed a restraining order against Sergio on January 13 because he owned twelve guns." At some point, I was put on the spot by either Slimelick or the clerk, and I was asked what I had posted. I admitted to posting Sergio's arraignment and the terms of his probation. Slimelick and the clerk agreed that that was not OK for me to do. I said, "Sergio's not safe to be around children, and the public should know that."

Slimelick asked me if I was the one behind the Rotten Fruit account. The clerk said I didn't have to answer any questions and reminded Slimelick he couldn't question me right now. Slimelick asked again anyways. I responded to Slimelick, saying, "I don't have to answer your questions." Before I knew it, my turn to speak was done, and the clerk had the floor once more.

The clerk said, "Based on what I've heard, I probably could find cause, but due to the circumstances, I'm continuing for six months. Do you have a criminal record?" I fucked up real bad right here. I answered no, which was a huge mistake. Slimelick interjected, saying I lied and had a DUI from thirteen years ago. It was true.

I do have a CWOF on my record from thirteen years ago. It happened three weeks after Sergio stole my camera at my wedding reception. My arrest and arraignment were publicly announced—my full name, age, address, crimes committed, loss of driver's license—all the details were printed online and in the newspaper. At one point you could even see my mug shot on the Hopkinton Police Department website if you searched my record. My dumb ass had gotten a DUI, so it was perfectly acceptable for the police and media to shame my ass for it.

But what I did, when I publicly announced Sergio's crime on social media, apparently that was different. According to the clerk and Sergio's attorney, what I did was wrong. Was I wrong? Or is Sergio so bad that he requires my silence for his own protection?

I still feel upset about making that mistake. I wish I would have answered yes, I do have a criminal record, like I should have. The clerk, however, did not seem phased by this interaction. He said, "I've heard your remarks, attorney. Regardless, I'm continuing six months. You are not to post about Sergio or the case on social media as part of the terms. Do you understand, Ms. Arvizu?"

"Yes." It's my duty to suffer in silence because speaking out elicits such a strong reaction from the public. Sergio's protection requires my silence, and this is a burden that I must carry. That's what I gathered from this continuation/silencing verdict.

Over at the courthouse, a bunch of family members were waiting for Sergio's criminal hearing to begin. I texted our family group chat with Trinny and the gang and said, "Zoom hearing did not go great. My case got continued six months. Tell Eric I'm fucking him up. He better stop fucking running his mouth." Stacey drove us up to the courthouse and dropped us off. Felipe and I proceeded downstairs to meet with the DA and victim-witness advocate. I was feeling defeated and traumatized, having been caught so completely off guard by Slimelick bombarding my hearing. I thought my hearing was going to be me versus Sergio. I thought the clerk was going to see through the bullshit.

The DA and victim-witness advocate walked in and asked us how my hearing went. I said, "Slimelick was there, and he was a fucking dickhead, and the clerk continued my case for six months. He said I can't post on social media! How can he silence me?!"

The DA and victim-witness advocate expressed sympathy toward me but explained there was nothing they could do to help me. The DA said only questionable people have a problem with what I said. I looked her dead in the face and said, "Well, the clerk just continued my case and silenced me for six months. So...the court thinks I did something wrong."

The DA agreed that was unfortunate, especially since the next thing she had to tell us was that Sergio's attorney was filing a motion, and there would be another hearing scheduled. Filing a motion means attorney Slimelick is requesting more records for Sergio's case. The DA explained that she wouldn't know the subject of the records request until two weeks before the hearing. She explained that they could be looking to access DCF or therapy records. Slimelick's new defense strategy was to go digging into our past, looking for dirt.

"So Slimelick and Sergio can continue to delay the case. All of a sudden, they need more records? What happened to Sergio pleading guilty? They can delay and distract and criminalize me, but I can't speak? This is fucked up!" The DA agreed the system was messed up and said it was mothers like me that changed laws and drove progress. How fucking dare she—to say that it's my responsibility to improve the system that employs her.

Felipe and I decided to go home that morning and not to attend Sergio's hearing. We later found out that Slimelick told the judge, "The mother of the victim has criminal harassment charges filed against her. And one of their friends nearly harassed my client this morning even though she isn't even present at this hearing." The judge told our friends and family members who were sitting in the courtroom not to say anything to the defendant or harass him in any way. The next hearing was scheduled for February 28, 2023.

We also found out exactly what Felipe's boyfriend said to Sergio that morning. When Eric saw Sergio, he asked him, "You're not wearing a face mask? You don't want to hide your face today?" How convenient for attorney Slimelick to have this fresh tea to spill on me as he manipulated the court schedule and snitched directly to the judge assigned to Sergio's case.

Eric was very upset when he found out this confrontation with Sergio made my court hearing worse. I knew he felt really badly about it, but I also knew I had to make it clear I was not ready to talk to him about it. I told Felipe, "You know I love Eric, but he can't go to court anymore. I get in enough trouble as it is. I do not need him adding fuel to the fire. He needs to shut the fuck up, or I'm gonna kick his ass. I get it though. Eric was just trying to be a good boyfriend."

The Right to Be Heard and Informed

I've been learning about victim-witness advocates. I stumbled upon this document called "The Massachusetts Victim-Witness Advocate Reference Manual." It's more than two hundred pages long and was published by the Massachusetts District Attorneys Association in 2010.

The introduction says, "Victim-witness advocates are professionals trained to support crime victims and witnesses. Victims and witnesses are guaranteed rights, services and protections under the law. Advocates have a duty to make sure that victims and witnesses get what they are entitled to. Advocates must also ensure all victims and witnesses are treated with compassion, dignity and fairness."

Reading this document is eye opening. The Massachusetts Victim Bill of Rights says we have a right to be informed. We have the right to be present at all court proceedings. We have the right to agree or to refuse to participate in interviews with the defense attorney, and we have the right to set reasonable conditions on such interviews.

Page seventeen of the document discusses media tips. It says, "Aside from M.G.L c. 265 s24C, which prohibits media from disseminating the names of sexual assault victims, no statute or common agreement constrains the media in publishing stories about crime."

Page eighteen offers advice to victims. It says, "Victims need to understand that they have certain privacy rights that they can enforce or relinquish." We can be as private or as loud as we want to be and can control how our story is presented.

Page nineteen goes on saying we have many rights, including the right to hire a spokesperson, exclude children and other family members from interviews, advance information on the angle of a story, completely give our side of the story, and suggest training about media and victims for print and electronic media in our community. There are many other rights afforded to victims and witnesses mentioned in this section.

Is it me, or did all my rights get completely violated at my magistrate hearing? I was questioned about why my family members would be at court and who was behind the Rotten Fruit account. I had to face Slimelick, Sergio's defense attorney, without any advance warning. My victim-witness advocate and the DA just looked the other way while I was left to fend for myself.

My understanding is that victims and witnesses have a right to share their stories as they see fit. It's about reclaiming your power as a survivor. It's part of the fucking healing process and shit. Exactly what statute constrains my social media accounts from reporting about crimes? We just read that there isn't one that constrains the regular media.

My victim-witness advocate isn't making sure we get what we are entitled to. It doesn't even feel like our basic rights as victims and witnesses are being upheld at all.

I may or may not have already gotten myself into more trouble, because six days after my hearing, I posted on social media. I did not mention Sergio by name or reference his case, so Felipe and I felt this post was safe-ish.

It was Tuesday, December 13, 2022, and I was trying to focus on my work, but I couldn't. Nothing could stop me from writing this poem and getting it off my chest. Then I posted it on Facebook. And shared it on the Rotten Fruit page. And made it into a TikTok with one of my flower drawings.

One year ago the truth was told
By a kid, so strong and bold
Always speak your truth my dear
Speak up loud for all to hear
Only criminals will take issue
Boo hoo perverts, grab a tissue

Stop telling me what I cannot do
It's not my fault people hate on you
You chose to commit the most heinous crimes
You hurt my family several times
In my brain, rotten thoughts fester
I might have a record, but you're a
CHILD MOLESTER

I also did more research about the rights of defendants awaiting trial for felony charges. Survivors have the right to be heard and informed. Sergio has the right to remain silent.

The Poetry Chapter

A lot has been happening in my actual life, so I haven't written a chapter in a while, but I have been writing some poetry. The first one I shared in the previous chapter was written on December 13, 2022—the one-year anniversary of the truth coming out. Here are some others.

December 26, 2022: I wrote this poem the day after Christmas. It's an acrostic poem.

The Perpetrator

Silence the mother
Exploit the truth
Restrict the justice
Groom the youth
Illegal desire
Obvious liar

Deliberately
Evil
Living his life
Gaslighting his wife
Avoiding the blame
Deferring the shame
Offenders don't want you to know their name.

January 27, 2023: I wrote this poem after receiving a restraining order from Sergio in the mail. My next court date was scheduled for February 2, 2023. Somewhere in the affidavit it says, "Erin directly violated her 6 month probationary anti-harassment order by making a Facebook post which included my name, various family members as well as the details regarding my wedding reception, which she wasn't invited to, showing she is stalking and harassing."

The Pedophile's Wife

A restraining order is a weird way to say
That I'm not invited to your wedding in May

Your commitment to this man
Is something I can't understand

A good accountant checks receipts
To unravel secrets that he keeps

He molested a child the whole time you were dating
Swallowing his lies must feel so degrading

But my opinion doesn't matter; you will do what
you choose
You seem to fit in nicely with this circus ring of fools

So have a blessed life
As the pedophile's wife

February 4, 2023: My lawyer submitted a motion to dismiss Sergio's restraining order against me, due to jurisdiction. Sergio lives in Gardner, Massachusetts, so if he wants a restraining order against me, by law he should be going to the Gardner District Court, not driving to Worcester to file one. As soon as attorney Slimelick read the motion, which was the day of my hearing, he told Sergio to withdraw the order. He said to the judge, "Sergio meant to file criminal harassment against Erin Arvizu, not a harassment prevention order. I gave him the wrong form."

Most recently I realized attorney Slimelick has a child at the same elementary school as my kids. I saw him one morning in the parent drop-off line.

The Pedophile's Lawyer

I know you took an oath to defend people like him,
Did he know who you were or select you on a whim?
I see the similarities in the way you think and act,
First you tell him to plead guilty, now the victim's
mother you attack.
You meant to file criminal harassment,
Not harassment prevention.
It feels like judicial harassment,
Is completely your intention.
Another day, another order,
Another notice to appear.
When retaliation is your only defense,
Your guilt speaks loud and clear..

March 3, 2023: I wrote this poem the day after the cops
showed up at Trinny's house. They were attempting to serve
Trevor with a restraining order from Ofelia. This was two days
after Sergio's court hearing was canceled due to a snowstorm.
The DA has not provided me with any updates regarding the
case, but my attorney filled me in. He said Sergio's next hearing will be April 27, 2023—two whole months away, and his
attorney will be filing a motion to suppress evidence—most
likely that police interview. He explained this is standard in the
legal world.

Delgado Low

What's lower than low?
Delgado Low,
The worst of all is Sergio.

The second worse is Ofelia.
His mother enables pedophilia.
A different kind of Delgado Low,
Also a known Restraining Order Hoe.

Two for him,
One for the mom.
Multiple perjuries all over the forms.

We are tired of the pain and the never-ending trauma,
No one loves extra court dates like the Pedophile and
his Mama.

I wrote this chapter on March 3, after I wrote that poem
and before the school called me. Right now, it feels like the calm
before the storm.

Sectioned

The school counselor called me around quarter of ten in the morning on Friday, March 3, 2023. She said Vinni came to see her. She didn't share any other details but said she wanted to call the mobile crisis team and set up a meeting for that day. Vinni was in agreement with speaking to the crisis team and said, "Mom, no offense, but you don't need to come to the school. I'll talk to the crisis people." The counselor explained to Vinni that I had to be at the school for the crisis team to come. He accepted the fact that I was coming.

I didn't exactly know what to expect, but if we were involving the crisis team, I knew it had something to do with suicidal ideation or self-harm. The crisis team called a little while later and set up a meeting for 1:00 p.m. I canceled my work appointments for the day. I took a shower, and I started drawing a picture. I finished coloring the whole page before I left for the meeting. I just had to outline it later.

I had already made plans to cook a prime rib that day. My mom had bought it back when they were on sale. Before I left for the meeting, I asked my parents if they could get the girls at the bus and left cooking instructions for the already-seasoned meat.

When I got to the school, I went into an office room where a teacher was working. I just sat quietly for the most part, bracing myself for how this meeting would unfold. The crisis team arrived, and there were three of them. Two women and one guy. They came to the office where I was sitting, and we began the meeting. Vinni was in another room, and I hadn't yet seen him.

The crisis team asked me some standard questions and explained the process. We would talk about what's been going on. They would make recommendations and assess the situation. The outcome would most likely be one of three things: outpatient services; CBAT, which is a residential-type placement that includes family therapy; or hospitalization. They also explained Section Twelve.

Section Twelve in the state of Massachusetts refers to the "emergency restraint and hospitalization of persons posing risk of serious harm by reason of mental illness." It means that an individual can be admitted to the hospital for at least three days without their consent or their guardian's consent.

After speaking to the crisis team, they said they were leaning mostly toward CBAT or hospitalization due to his age and other circumstances. They asked me how I felt about this. I said I wanted what was best for my son and would do whatever they deemed to be the best for Vinni. Then the guy left our meeting and went to talk to Vinni.

Vinni seemed comfortable with the crisis guy and told the counselor it was fine if she wanted to leave. The remaining crisis team members had me fill out paperwork, and they answered whatever questions I might have. At dismissal time, the crisis team guy came running into our office saying, "Vinni just left for bus dismissal!" We all ran down the hall to get him—the meeting was not finished yet.

Vinni absolutely did not want to do parent pickup that day. He protested leaving the bus line. He cried and yelled. It took a few minutes of talking to him to convince him to agree to go back and finish the meeting with the crisis team. I told him I would drive us home later, that there was no bus for him that day.

He was very angry but eventually agreed to leave the bus line. He took off very quickly and tried to bolt out a side door at the school. The custodian, along with the crisis team, counselor and the principal caught up to Vinni and got him back into the counselor's office. The crisis team convened in the office, waiting for the psychiatrist to call them back.

Vinni was fucking pissed. He immediately went over to the bulletin board section of the room and started pulling tacks out of the wall. He took scotch tape and taped the tacks to a gum container, sharp side up.

He found two pairs of scissors in that office. The counselor wrestled one pair away from him. I pried a second pair out of his fingers. He grabbed a blunt wooden stick from the fidget-toy box and started sharpening it in a pencil sharpener. It was taken from him too. He told the counselor he knows how to remove the blade of a sharpener to use it for self-harm. I heard that for the first time that day. It felt like hours we waited—the counselor, principal, Vinni, and I, just trying to keep him safe in a seemingly normal school office room that was actually quite dangerous for a kid like him in that moment.

The crisis team eventually told me, "We are doing the Section Twelve." I agreed to the hospitalization. An ambulance came. I abandoned my car and rode in the back with him. We were brought to the emergency room of a local hospital. This was my second ER experience of 2023. Just a couple months ago, I was in the ER with Felipe. He is now on heart rate meds, blood pressure meds, in addition to the cholesterol meds, but he is healthy otherwise.

Vinni did not like the woman who sat in the back of the ambulance, but I thought she was great! She was very honest and blunt. As he was laying on the stretcher, he asked for no siren during the ride, and the EMTs were cool about it. The EMT also gave him some gauze for his ears in case the ride still felt too noisy.

He got pissed at me at one point and threw the gauze at me. The EMT said, "That was really rude." He shot her a reaction with a face and voice that said I'm just kid! Don't talk to me like that! She held her ground and responded with, "It was rude, bro! You just whipped the gauze at your mom. Your mom's just trying to help you."

It's weird riding in the back of an ambulance. I couldn't tell where we were just from looking out the back window. The EMT said that was something she had to learn on the job—to navigate the city of Worcester from the back-view window. As the driver EMT backed into the hospital ER unloading zone, I asked if there were a ton of backup cameras on this thing. She said, "Oh yeah, there's a camera on us, so the driver can see what we're doing back here with the patient. Also, there's tons of cameras on the outside too."

I recently took off my mirror just backing out of my garage. And I had three kids sitting in the back, so I couldn't even pretend to Felipe that I didn't know what happened. I could never be the ambulance driver, backing that up dozens of times per shift.

When we arrived at the hospital, strict instructions were given to the receiving nurse. Vinni was self-injurious and a flight risk and required one-on-one observation at all times. Being a child in the psych ward of the ER meant he got a room right away. They took his shoes and his sweatshirt because they had strings. I also had to surrender my belongings, including my cell phone—that was the hospital rule for the psych ward section of the ER.

Vinni was pissed about being in the hospital. The room had two doors, one on either side across from each other; however one was locked from both sides. He could not open it from the inside, and no one could open it from the other side, which was the adult section of the psych ward in the ER. Throughout our overnight stay in that room, we heard moaning and yelling from the other patients on the other side. Patients would also try to open the door sometimes before being brought back to their rooms.

There was a section of the room that had cabinet doors that had been removed, so it now looked like two small cubby sections. Vinni immediately went in there. He said, "Hey Mom, guess what it says in here? Ari is a pussy-ass bitch." He started laughing. He found three other messages about Ari.

We talked about who Ari might be and what the heck happened to make this person hate her so much. The nurse that was sitting in the doorway observing us said she never knew there was writing in there. Only a child would crawl in to hang out in there.

After a few hours, we got some dinner. I thought about my family back at home and how they were eating prime rib. Vinni and I each had a turkey sandwich that consisted of exactly one piece of turkey and two pieces of white bread. Vinni asked for a second one after devouring the first. He said to me, "At least the food is really good here." He had already had ice cream and apple juice as well.

I had to go to the desk in the ER hallway to use the phone and call Felipe. I still didn't really know what the plan was. We were waiting for a member of the crisis team to come evaluate Vinni and determine the next step. They also had collected a urine and blood sample from him. And a COVID-19 test.

Being small does have its benefits. Vinni and I were both able to sleep on the one bed in the ER hospital room. I was so exhausted that I actually did get a few naps in that night, despite the bright lights, constant ER noises, and psych ward moaning. Oh, we also got a snowstorm that night. Sergio's court date got canceled due to snow and postponed for an entire two whole months, but absolutely nothing was stopping our Section Twelve that night or the snowy transport to the next hospital the following morning.

I called Felipe again around 7:40 a.m. the next morning. It was Saturday. He was home alone with the cats. The girls were staying at my parents' house. "Hey, how are you? Do you want me to come there?"

"Hi babe." I explained what I knew so far. "We are still waiting for the crisis team people to come talk to us, so I don't really know what the plan is yet. But I am wicked tired and want to go home. Could you come here and stay with him for a few hours while I go home and shower and stuff?"

"Yes! I just have to shovel a little bit." Oh yeah, eight-plus inches was the forecast for Worcester that day. Vinni was still tired, but he was in good spirits. We received our breakfast bags, and he asked if I was going to eat my yogurt. After he housed the cereal, blueberry muffin, two yogurts, his and my granola bar, and a ginger ale, I told him Dad was coming to hang out with him for a little bit, and I was going home. He was fine with that and looked forward to seeing Felipe.

When I got home, I made a coffee, changed out of the hospital clothes, into jammies, and snuggled with my cats in my bed. Then I called Stacey. She wasn't busy, just hanging out with her family. I told her about our ER psych ward stay and how Felipe was at the hospital with Vinni. She choked up a little at one point and shared how she had a rough week as well. She said, "How about I come over and we just hang out?"

"Yes." My immediate response. "And we just watch TV?" She said of course. I then asked, "Can you bring Dunkin' Donuts or McDonald's? I haven't eaten anything but hospital food since yesterday." She said absolutely, and we decided on McDonald's. I went back and forth between nuggets or a cheeseburger. I told her, "I'll just text you my order, but most likely it will be nuggets with sweet-and-sour sauce."

Stacey later had to gently break the news to me that it was still breakfast time at McDonalds, and so I had to forfeit both the burger and nuggets for breakfast items. "Two hash browns and a bacon, egg, and cheese, please." After updating my order, I received a text from Felipe reminding me that Olivia had softball tryouts that afternoon. He still had his cell phone in the ER. That lucky duck didn't get his stuff locked up like I did. I had to ask for special permission to retrieve my ChapStick from my bag. And when I needed a pad because I unexpectedly got my period that night...in the ER pysch ward with zero belongings on me.

I called my mom, and she reassured me that my dad was taking Olivia to softball. I filled her in about Vinni, our overnight stay in the ER, and how we were still waiting to hear about next steps. Then Felipe started beeping in, so I switched over to his phone call.

Felipe said, "They have a bed in Devens. It's another hospital, so Vinni started freaking out and yelling and saying he wants to go home. I guess they are gonna bring him by ambulance to the new place. Like, what should I do? Should I come home to get the car and follow the ambulance?"

"No. Go in the ambulance with him," I said. "Just try to explain that these people are the experts, and in order to keep him safe, we have to go to the next hospital, which will be better than the ER. I can figure out if I can pack a bag of his stuff and whatnot. When you get to the new place, we will figure out the next plan of me coming to get you and bringing his stuff."

Then someone from the hospital was calling me and beeping in, so I ended the call with Felipe to talk to that person. It was a member of the crisis team explaining how a bed opened up at a place in Devens. I had a bunch of questions, but she walked me through everything. After three days they would see how he was doing and decide if he could step down to CBAT, which is the residential place with family therapy. If not, he may be at Devens for five to seven days, but it will be based on him. I got off the phone with her feeling relieved. He was getting the help he needed. It was out of my hands, in the best way possible. It was Felipe's turn to do the ambulance ride while I ate McDonald's with Stacey.

We weren't out of the woods yet. Felipe was not allowed to go with Vinni inside the Devens hospital. He would have to say goodbye to Vinni in the ambulance. There was so much change in such a short period of time, and now we were leaving our kid with complete strangers. After Stacey and I ate our McDonald's, I took a shower and packed a big bag for Vinni, including his snow gear.

At one point, while we were still in the ER, Vinni angrily compared the hospital to prison. "I have no privacy! This is so unfair! I'm trapped against my will. It's like prison!" I just sat there on the chair with my mask on while he finished his rant. I was tired and overwhelmed and had already been at the hospital for hours. Then he asked, "Do I get yard time here?"

The nurse said, "Hey, this is not a prison. It's a hospital to keep you safe. And no there is no yard here." I'm glad he was getting yard time at the new place. When I arrived at the new hospital with Stacey, the ambulance had just arrived, and Felipe was there waiting for us. I went to the reception area with Vinni's stuff, but they told me I could bring it to him at our first visit.

She said she had a time slot available at 4:40 p.m. that afternoon. I signed myself and Felipe up for our first visitation.

We drove the half hour home. Then we made plans for our next half-hour drive to go see him, where we would be able to visit with him for thirty minutes. That was how we would be seeing our son for the next few days or however long he stayed there. I outlined the drawing I started the day before, and I included it in Vinni's things, so he would have something colorful to put up in his new room.

Vinni called me around 3:00 p.m. and said, "Mom, this place is actually awesome! I have like ten new friends. Anyways, I have to go so I'll talk to you later. I love you!" My heart sang with joy to know he was happy at his new hospital. Something that started out so traumatic and unsure was settling at a place where he felt good. For the first time, he was connecting with other kids who were struggling, like him. He wasn't different; he was just going to heal alongside them. The tower fell on Friday, but on Saturday we started to rebuild.

I actually did pull the tower card that Friday, just after the school counselor called to set up the meeting. For anyone who does tarot, you can understand my gut reaction to pulling the tower in this moment, but seeing the nine of pentacles on the bottom of the deck did give me some feeling of hope. It would be scary, but it would be successful in the end. And that's how this Section Twelve experience feels right now.

Trevor Speaks Up

Last year, when Ofelia and Estela filed their restraining orders against Trevor, he had to vacate 32 Arthur Street as soon as the police served the orders. As a result, he moved into my house with limited belongings, with about a day's notice. We set up an air mattress in the dining room temporarily until we figured out how long he would be staying.

I remember talking to Trevor before his hearing about a plan to stay at my house regardless of the restraining order outcome. He had been living with us for about a week or so, and I brought him up to the attic, where we have two additional bedrooms. Felipe had to do a little work to make sure the room had heat and light. And we had to move some stuff out since we had just been using it as storage, but it was a much better space than the dining room.

"It might be a little scary up here with the bats and the ghosts, but at least you will have your own room with a door, away from the first-floor ruckus. Even if the judge terminates the orders tomorrow, you should just stay here until your mom moves, so the Delgados can't fuck with you." I showed Trevor the room with the shag carpet. It is to the right once you come up the attic stairs. Felipe took the stairwell door off so he would have better temperature regulation and airflow. It also made the attic space feel more like a part of our home and not just a storage area upstairs. It became Trevor's room.

Felipe helped him get his TV and gaming system from Trinny's house so Trevor had a nice little space up in the attic. It was furnished with random paintings, curtains, and artwork made by us Arvizus. Vinni and I also gave him some crystals to help the energy up there. I'm not exaggerating about the bats and ghosts. My house was built in 1912 and has been owned by several families. A psychic came to my house once and said there was a lot of spirit activity in my attic—generations of ghosts were tied to their childhood home. She also said there were a lot of spirits congregating in Vinni's bedroom. She came to my house on November 13, 2021, one month before Vinni spoke his truth.

The first time I encountered a bat was back when I was pregnant with Luna in 2017. I woke up in the middle of the night to something flying overhead. I didn't quite know what it was at first—a bird or a big-ass bug? Then I realized it was a bat. I nudged Felipe awake and said, "I think there's a bat flying in our room!"

"What?" Felipe groggily responded, still half asleep, and rolled over. "Are you sure it's not a bug?" he sleepily mumbled. Then the flying object swooped down right in front of Felipe's face. He shrieked and said, "That's a fucking bat!"

"I know! What do we do?!"

"Here, take my chancla," he said, as he handed me his flip-flop. "Use this as protection while I run upstairs to the attic." Did he actually think I was going to murder the bat with his chancla? As soon as Felipe left the room, the bat flew into our bathroom. I slammed the door shut and trapped it. Felipe came back downstairs with a boat paddle in his hands. I didn't quite understand his weapon choices, but there was no time to question him. I said, "I did my part and trapped it for you. You just have to kill it." But here in Massachusetts, you can't kill bats, because they're a protected species.

Felipe went into the bathroom, armed with his boat paddle. He opened the window and hit the bat outside. There wasn't a body in the yard the next day. Therefore he didn't kill it. About a year later, we had another bat experience. Another middle-of-the-night visit from a flying creature, where I woke Felipe up and told him, "Go get your boat paddle—we have another fucking bat in our room."

Trevor liked living in the attic and was appreciative. He said the bats and ghosts never bothered him. He also agreed to stay at my house regardless of the restraining order outcome. It would be a better environment for him. The Delgados wouldn't try to attack him if he lived here, and he wouldn't be tempted to fight them if he never saw them. The day of his restraining order hearings, we were unprepared, inexperienced defendants. And we were facing the Restraining Order Hoe herself. I didn't have a copy of the affidavit. I didn't know what they were going to show for evidence. I didn't help him prepare a response. I advised him about what to say, and I said he should try to say as little as possible and let Ofelia look like the crazy one. We just showed up at the hearing that morning and hoped for the best.

The judge ended up extending both Ofelia's and Estela's restraining orders. It was infuriating, but at least we had a living arrangement plan in place, regardless. He had a stable home to live in while Trinny did some house hunting.

When February 2023 rolled around, Ofelia and Estela received letters from the courthouse reminding them that their restraining orders were expiring, and if they wanted them extended, they had to go back to court. They ended up missing the extension dates, so they went to the clerk and filed new restraining orders against Trevor. The cops showed up at Trinny's new house looking for him.

Trinny was livid. Trevor hadn't seen or spoken to any of the Delgados in over a year. He wasn't talking smack about them on social media. He was not even staying at Trinny's house—he had been staying at a new girlfriend's house. Why the fuck did Ofelia and Estela need to file more restraining orders against him?

I called Trevor and asked him to send me the documents once he got them from the courthouse and police station. I offered to help him write a response and said I would go to the hearing with him if he wanted me to. That day came, and the morning of March 16, 2023, I drove Olivia and Luna to school, then picked up Trevor, and off to court we went.

I paid to park across the street because it was already 8:45 a.m., and I didn't want to walk far in the shoes I was wearing. We made our way through security and checked in at the annex. Trevor's hearing was in courtroom 24. I stopped at the bathroom, and then we took the elevator up to the fourth floor. We sat down on a bench in the lobby. It was 8:58 a.m. Usually, the doors open to the court, and an officer tells you to come in. The crowd goes in and takes their seats. We waited and waited, but the court doors never opened. Courtroom 23 opened next door, and a bunch of people went inside. Why wasn't courtroom 24 open yet? I went up to the door and looked in but didn't see a judge. This was weird, we thought. No Delgado sightings, and it's past ten, and no court yet.

I walked over to the restroom and as I was about to enter, I saw Ofelia and Estela exit courtroom 24. Fuck. We fucked up. Court is in session, and we've been in the lobby area the whole time like dumbasses! I went back over to Trevor and said, "I just saw Ofelia and Estela come out of the courtroom. We gotta go in there! Court is in session, and we missed your hearing!"

Trevor and I walked into the courtroom. The court officer asked who he was and what he was here for. Trevor said his name and that he was there for a restraining order hearing. The judge angrily responded with, "My court opens at nine. I already heard that case at 10:24 a.m. It's too late. You should have been on time to court."

"I'm sorry!" The little white girl had to do something. I stepped out from behind tall Trevor and his box braids and said, "We were here at 9:00 a.m. and were waiting in the lobby area. Usually, when we come to restraining order hearings, someone comes and opens the doors when court starts, and we all go in. We were waiting in the lobby. I'm sorry." The judge glared at me as he sighed and told us to take a seat. We immediately sat down and faced forward. He then called down to the annex, asking for Ofelia and Estela Delgado to come back upstairs to the courtroom because the other party had arrived.

We had one more shot at his hearing, but we were already off to a rocky start. We were late, and the judge hated us. But we were armed—and not with a boat paddle or chancla. Trevor had a typed response ready to read aloud and a copy of the police report I filed back in December reporting Ofelia's perjury at my restraining order session—proof she is a liar.

Ofelia and Estela made their way back inside the courtroom. The clerk called Trevor's case, and both parties took the stands. Ofelia and Estela shared the same sob story as last time. That

Trevor threatened them and does drugs and has domestic violence charges. They showed screenshots from Facebook and cried at the end to show how scared they are of him.

Then it was Trevor's turn to speak. He cleared his throat and read his response. He did a great job speaking his truth, sticking up for himself, and kicking Delgado ass.

"Your Honor, the last time I spent time with my aunt Ofelia and her family was on Thanksgiving in 2021. She references an incident that occurred on September 26, 2021, in her affidavit. She claims I tried to hurt her on this day, yet she was not fearful of me two months later when we gathered as a family for the Thanksgiving holiday.

"My cousin Sergio Delgado, Ofelia's son, was formally charged with two counts of indecent assault and battery on a minor under fourteen years of age on February 16, 2022. My little cousin told their mom that Sergio had been sexually abusing them since they were four years old. Around that time, I saw my aunt Ofelia in the hallway because I was living with my mother on the third floor of 32 Arthur Street. I told Ofelia to stay away from my family. I have young children I need to protect. I never told anyone when I was a kid, but Sergio sexually abused me as well. I know what he is capable of, and I know Ofelia will enable the abuse. After this interaction with Ofelia, both she and Estela filed restraining orders against me.

"Once the restraining orders were served in February 2022, I had to vacate my childhood home immediately. I moved in with my aunt, where I lived until June 2022. In June 2022, I moved into a new home with my mother since she no longer resided at 32 Arthur Street. The Delgado family enabled Sergio to sexually abuse four of us in their home. I was one of them. My brother and sister also suffered abuse by Sergio. We all carry the effects of this abuse in different ways. Ofelia speaks about my drug use and mental health issues on her paperwork. I am not perfect. I have four young girls I'm trying to be a good father to. I struggle with demons inside of me due to the trauma Sergio inflicted.

"Ofelia Delgado has filed several restraining orders against me and my family. Most recently she filed one against my aunt Erin Arvizu, the mother of my little cousin who has filed charges against Sergio. The judge terminated the restraining order on December 2, 2022. Ofelia's affidavit was full of lies, as well as her spoken testimony. My aunt filed a police report on December 5, 2022 for perjury against Ofelia. I have a copy of this police report as evidence.

"My family and I want nothing to do with Ofelia Delgado or her family. They enable child sexual abuse. They protect sexual predators. And they retaliate against us every chance they get. My mother and my aunt have both felt the trauma of the police coming to their homes delivering these orders. And I was already kicked out of my residence last year. My mother and grandmother both moved out of their homes to distance themselves from the Delgados. We do not communicate with them or go anywhere near their home. I am asking you to please terminate these orders and put a stop to this recurring judicial abuse.

"Thank you, Your Honor."

Ofelia and Estela gasped at certain times while Trevor was speaking. Ofelia was completely unaware I had filed a police report against her. She also claimed there was no distance between her and her mother. She said they talk every day, and the only reason Carmen moved away was because we were all feeding her lies. She also brought up my TikTok videos and how she fears for her granddaughter. She even used the "murder thoughts comment" from my Facebook.

Estela joined in too. She said she feared for her safety because she knows how Trevor can be. At the end, as a last ditch effort, she started crying as she said, "Trevor's mother, Trinny, came to my work earlier this week. I felt so scared! I feared for my safety because I was so worried Trevor might be there in the car in the parking lot." Estela works at an urgent care facility. She violated HIPAA on record while she lied about the fear she felt toward Trevor. That's a new Delgado Low.

The judge asked Ofelia repeatedly if her son Sergio did in fact have an active legal case with Erin Arvizu, and she said, "No, not that I'm aware of." I did not speak out of turn. I just sat in the audience while the Delgados dug their own grave.

The judge then said, "After hearing both parties, I am terminating both orders. There is no sufficient evidence of threats or abuse." Ofelia and Estela stormed out of the courtroom mumbling under their breath as they walked by me. I sat with my head facing forward. Then Trevor came and sat next to me. He was smiling ear to ear. The judge then exited, and the clerk handed us the paperwork showing that both restraining orders were terminated.

I'm proud of Trevor. He showed up, and he spoke his truth. Even that cranky judge who hated us for being late could see right through those gross Delgados. I wish I had time to take Trevor out to eat to celebrate, but it's tax season, and I had to rush back to work after court. Then I picked up Illianna, and we went to visit Vinni in the hospital. On the way to the hospital, the mental health department called me to discuss the plan for Vinni's services.

It's been two weeks since my Vinni slept at my home. I don't know when he will be coming home.

Award-Winning Child Abuse

On April 6, 2023, the Worcester County District Attorney recognized a team of local professionals specifically trained to aid and care for victims of child abuse and their families. This team was presented with the District Attorney's Team Excellence and Merit Award for their unwavering work in serving the children of Worcester County and their families. April is also known as National Child Abuse Prevention Month. My friend Kerri enlightened me one Saturday while I was at work.

As I read the article about the award-winning child abuse prosecutors, my blood began to boil, and I almost lost my goddamn fucking mind. "Are these the people that work on your case?" Kerri asked as she forwarded me the link with the article.

The Worcester County District Attorney is quoted in the article saying, "Victims of child abuse and trauma, along with their families, reach out to be heard in the most difficult times. This group of professionals are here to help, offering a listening ear and a range of services to seek justice and start the healing journey."

Who are these award-winning professionals? The day before this article was released, my victim-witness advocate emailed me. She is a member of this award-winning team. She wrote, "Hi Erin, I am sending along some information provided by the family advocate, per the request from your attorney on our last Zoom call." When I clicked the link she sent, it brought me to mental health and counseling resources.

That Zoom call she mentioned was about a week ago. The virtual meeting consisted of me, my victim-witness advocate, the DA assigned to my case, and my attorney. Even though our case has been in existence for over a year now, this was the first time I had a meeting like this. Usually, I only see my victim-witness advocate and the DA at Sergio's court hearings when we talk to them in the victim chambers.

During the zoom call, the DA said to me, "We think the trial may be scheduled for this fall. Erin, do you think Vinni will be OK to testify by then?"

I took a deep breath as I explained, "That's hard for me to gauge. Vinni has been hospitalized for almost a month now and is still suicidal." The DA expressed sadness toward that news. Then she explained that if Vinni wasn't ready to testify in the fall, she could hold the case and postpone the trial. But without

Vinni's testimony, there was no case. This did not make any fucking sense to me! "But the whole reason why Vinni is too traumatized to testify is because of Sergio! Vinni is suicidal and can't live at home with me—his own mother—because of what Sergio did to him!" The DA agreed the system was messed up. She reiterated how moms like me can change it. She confirmed that I'm not the only one pissed about the circumstances, but rules are rules.

It feels completely unethical for the system to require a child victim to testify, regardless of retraumatization. No testimony from Vinni, no sex offender registry and no jail time for Sergio. If Vinni is too traumatized to testify, Sergio will be off the hook, free to abuse more children, under the radar. This is the opposite of preventing child abuse—it's enabling it. The system enables child abuse when the child victim is too traumatized to testify.

On this Thursday, April 6, 2023, before I even knew these people were "award winning," I spoke to my attorney on the phone about how angry and hurt I felt. I had just finished visiting with Vinni when my lawyer called. We talked for the whole drive back to Worcester, and he spent a great deal of time advising me to stop posting on social media in order to minimize my chances of being charged with a crime.

At one point I asked him, "How come Attorney Slimelick can act like a dickhead at court and not get in trouble?"

My attorney responded with, "I don't know. Because he's a lawyer, I guess?"

"And only lawyers can act like dicks. Moms have to be completely silent. He can say whatever he wants to the judge and talk shit about the victim's mother, but I can't speak out about my trauma on social media. I can't say shit, even though everything is completely fucked up! EVERYTHING!" I cried. I felt angry and helpless. My attorney said no one sues the DA and wins. They have absolute immunity.

Then I pissed off my lawyer when I confessed how I had impulsively invited the Massachusetts Attorney General to my criminal harassment hearing. "You did WHAT?!?"

I cried some more and told my attorney I didn't want to be quiet and follow the rules. The rules don't help my family. The system was failing families like mine and kids like Vinni. "Moms like me have to dismantle the system!"

My attorney didn't break up with me. However he made it abundantly clear that it was in my best interest to shut the fuck up and stop emailing people.

It's unfathomable to me that the burden of bringing Sergio to justice weighs on my nine-year-old's shoulders, not the system's. The system is unable to prove that Sergio is a sexual predator, regardless of the fact that four victims have come forward, the perpetrator made a confession to the police, and there's a paper trail of retaliation against us. If Sergio were genuinely innocent, attorney Slimelick would have a better defense strategy besides threatening me to the judge.

When my friend Kerri sent me that article about the award-winning child abuse prosecutors the Saturday before Easter, I nearly lost my shit completely. After I vented to her about my actual experiences with these professionals and the real-life circumstances my family faces, my friend asked me, "How do these people sleep at night, thinking they're doing the right thing?"

"Not on a bare mattress in the mental hospital, like my nine-year-old child does—that's for sure." That was the only response I could muster before my busy day of clients began. Last year Trevor couldn't go home for Easter because of the Restraining Order Hoe. This year Vinni can't be home for Easter because of the Fucking Pervert. When will Easter start getting fucked up for the Restraining Order Hoe and the Fucking Pervert?

My family's over here experiencing life on the inside at the child victim level, while the perpetrator lives a normal life, benefiting from snow days, court delays, and the unbearable trauma he inflicted.

Life on the Inside

Two razor blades and nine restraints
Daily cheeking med complaints
Code gray
Attempted escape
Thirty-minute visit

Two-person limit
Injection medication
Mental stabilization
Shards of plastic on the floor
Secrets can't hide any more.

While the award-winning child abuse professionals celebrate Easter with their loved ones, I hope they are aware of what this experience is like for the actual victims they serve. In lieu of giving Vinni a proper Easter with a basket and egg hunt, I drew him a picture of a daffodil surrounded by crocuses and grape hyacinth flowers. On the back of the drawing, I wrote this poem:

Easter Showers

Three months and three days,
Then everything changed.
Now marks month four,
April flowers, miss you more.
Feel my hug as you read this,
Let my love fill your heart,
You are my life and my family,
You are a beautiful work of art.

And this poem is for the award-winning child abuse prosecutors:

Fuck you
Fuck you
None of you are cool.

Cinco de Full Moon

When Vinni was admitted to the acute behavioral hospital in Devens, Massachusetts, we were told most kids stay there for around ten days, but his actual length of stay would depend upon Vinni's progress. Once discharged, Vinni would continue outpatient therapy, and the Department of Mental Health (DMH) would be aiding our family during this transition. Vinni arrived at the Devens hospital on March 4, 2023. His first outpatient therapy session was initially scheduled for March 30, assuming he would be ready for discharge by the end of the month.

I immediately contacted my attorney. The magistrate hearing for my second criminal harassment charge from Sergio had already been scheduled for March 30, 2023. But now this day was committed to Vinni's first session with the new therapist. I asked my lawyer to file a motion requesting a court date change.

He asked me which day I wanted it changed to. I said May 5, Cinco de Mayo.

A few months prior, my family and I were at Disney World on vacation. The morning we went to Epcot Center, I discovered something disturbing. I don't know why I decided to research this on vacation, but I did. I googled "Becca and Sergio Delgado wedding" and immediately stumbled upon Becca's personal wedding website through theknot.com. I read all about their upcoming wedding reception. It was scheduled for May 6, 2023, in Barre, MA. It listed Mia's father as the groom's best man. Mia was listed as the flower girl.

Reading this information triggered me. The clerk at my first magistrate hearing continued my case for six months and told me not to talk about Sergio or his case on social media. Attorney Slimelick told the judge assigned to Sergio's criminal case that the magistrate found cause at my hearing and if I posted one more thing on social media, Sergio and his attorney would be right back here to file more orders.

I emailed the DA saying everything makes sense now. They silenced me so the pedophile could have a nice wedding. I included a link to their wedding site. Per usual, the DA's office did not respond to my communication. Then, the morning we were at the airport about to fly home, my Facebook memories reminded me of my original post from January 13, 2022. This was the meme that said, "Never seek revenge, rotten fruit falls by itself." Then I posted my affidavit on social media and called out the magistrate clerk. I asked my followers, "You guys will fill up my canteen if I get locked up first, right? The clerk told me to be quiet, but clearly I won't be quiet, not for a pedophile or a fucked system."

This ultimately led to my second criminal harassment charge from Sergio. A letter from the courthouse arrived in the mail exactly one week after I made that announcement. As soon as I grabbed that letter out of my mailbox, the school counselor called. She said she wanted to talk to me about something. She said two parents of students in Vinni's class had contacted her that week with concerns that Vinni was self-harming. The counselor explained to the parents that both she and I were aware of the self-harming.

When Vinni got home from school that day, I confronted him. I said, "Hey Vinni. Mrs. Petty called me earlier to talk to me about something. She said some kids in your class have noticed the cuts on your arms and told their parents, and they called the school saying they are concerned about you."

"I'm sorry, Mom!" Vinni broke down sobbing and apologized repeatedly. "I didn't mean for the other kids to say anything about it. I'm sorry." He continued crying.

I told him it wasn't his fault, and he wasn't in trouble. I said no one was mad at him. I told him I loved him and wanted him to be OK. I said "The thing is, we can all see the cuts on your arms. A lot of people, including me, are very concerned. We can face this head on and say something to your class, like 'Vinni is dealing with something hard,' but not actually talk about what we are dealing with, just ask for respect and privacy. I think we should also work on reducing and stopping the self-harming." Vinni agreed to try to reduce the self-harming but did not want to say anything to his class. This was about four months ago when Vinni lived with us.

Our motion requesting to move my hearing to Friday, May 5, 2023, was approved. Happy Cinco de Mayo, Sergio—see you at court on the eve of your wedding. A couple months later, we filed another motion requesting to have an in-person hearing instead of a Zoom hearing like last time. If all of Sergio's hearings are in person and all the same players show up each time, why do mine have to be on Zoom?

The motion stated:

"The unique circumstances of this case warrant an in-person hearing, in the interests of justice.

1. Ms. Arvizu is a 39-year-old mother of three children with no criminal record;
2. Mr. Delgado is currently charged with sexually abusing Ms. Arvizu's 9-year-old son. In that case, which is pending, Ms. Arvizu is a first complaint witness who would testify against Mr. Delgado at trial;
3. Since Mr. Delgado was charged, Mr. Delgado has initiated an unsuccessful civilian application for criminal harassment against Ms. Arvizu and an unsuccessful civil harassment prevention order application against Ms. Arvizu;
4. Additionally, after Mr. Delgado was charged, Mr. Delgado's mother initiated an unsuccessful civil harassment prevention order against Ms. Arvizu;
5. This latest attempt by Mr. Delgado to use the criminal justice system against a witness against him marks the fourth time Ms. Arvizu will be brought to court to respond to allegations by Mr. Delgado, or his mother, since Ms. Arvizu's son was abused;
6. The convenience that the virtual hearing bestows on most litigants is, at this point, likely being abused by Mr. Delgado,

who is permitted as a civilian applicant to bring Ms. Arvizu before the court, yet again, without having to leave the comfort of his home;

7. Furthermore, because the credibility of Mr. Delgado, and particularly his motives and biases in testifying, will be critical to the court's determination of this matter, Ms. Arvizu respectfully requests that this Honorable Court allow her the opportunity to have an in-person hearing."

This was the official response from the Worcester District Court. Moms like me are a public safety issue.

"Thank you for your motion for an in-person hearing for the upcoming show cause hearing with your client. As you may know, I was the Magistrate who heard the initial request for a harassment order against Ms. Arvizu on December 7, 2022.

My review of the record indicates that I found sufficient facts for probable cause against Ms. Arvizu, but continued the matter under SFF35A to June 6th, 2023, for compliance and dismissal. Both parties were understandably emotional and upset throughout the proceeding. I believe that an in-person hearing would only exacerbate that anger and would not be in the best interest of justice or public safety.

For those reasons, the motion is denied."

My attorney said this denial for an in-person hearing wasn't the end of the world, and we still had a good defense. I told him I wanted to fuck shit up and contact the media. He said maybe we should start with a scalpel, not a sledgehammer. I asked for the sledgehammer again.

My attorney said his best advice was for me to take down my social media accounts immediately. Then we would go to court and apologize for calling out the clerk. Then we would say we took down all social media accounts and will not post anymore. He explained our uphill battles. It was most likely going to be the same clerk hearing my case again. My lawyer explained how on average 83 percent of magistrate hearings move forward as criminal complaints in Worcester District Court. I was already in the 17 percent that did not move forward once. Now I needed to be there again, up against the same clerk as last time. I still wasn't doing it. Doing that felt icky. I did not break the law. Sergio did. I'm not apologizing for speaking, and I'm not taking down my social media accounts.

I have the right to fuck shit up by speaking. I also realized that May 5 was the full moon—the flower full moon. This made me feel optimistic. Full moons are for endings and letting go. It was absolutely the perfect day to release what is no longer serving me. I told my lawyer not to worry, fuck shit up a little. He wrote a memorandum of law. I collected four character reference letters and obtained letters from DMH and the hospital where Vinni was staying. My attorney submitted all this documentation to the magistrate clerk before my hearing.

There was one last thing we had to work out. My attorney said, "When it comes to legal strategy, it's up to the lawyer, but when it comes to testifying, that is 100 percent a client's decision. I am advising you not to testify, but if you disagree, we will change that." I told him I was perfectly fine with being silent at my hearing, knowing full well it would benefit me to shut the fuck up for once. Also, my resting bitch face speaks for itself.

The day of court, Felipe and I drove into Boston to my attorney's office. We hit a little traffic, parked a little far away, and stepped into my lawyer's office at 8:57 a.m. for a 9:00 a.m. hearing. I had exactly one minute to decompress once I logged on into the Zoom courtroom. Felipe carried my box of emotional support cookies from Crumbl and set them on the counter nearby. I didn't have a moment to eat though. My hearing was called first thing that morning.

I sat on my laptop with my audio muted, while my attorney sat across from me on his laptop. He would mute his audio whenever he asked me a question. Sergio did not appear on camera at first. He called in on his phone. The clerk asked him if the phone he was speaking on had a camera and then asked him to log on through Zoom like we all had done. Sergio said his laptop wasn't working earlier—that's why he called in. But as we all sat there, Sergio restarted his laptop. He also explained how attorney Slimelick was not going to be representing him at this hearing. His laptop started working because he popped up on screen a few moments later.

My lawyer totally kicked his ass that day. I thoroughly enjoyed hearing Sergio read my poetry aloud and admit on record that he was scared of a four-foot-eleven woman physically harming him at his wedding. He said because of me he received a threatening Facebook message. He had no evidence that this person was connected to me in any way, but he said he had to hire extra security for his wedding.

My attorney held up a picture I sent him from Becca's Facebook. It's two pictures of Becca and Sergio side by side, each holding big ass machine guns, and the caption says, "Can you tell we're soul mates? Lmfao." Sergio confirmed that he recognized the picture and said that was posted years ago. He also confirmed that once he was served with his restraining orders, the police confiscated his and Becca's guns.

My attorney called Sergio out on relentlessly trying to charge me with a crime in order to help with his own defense in his criminal case. Sergio's response to that was, "My attorney said at this point, that wouldn't even help my case." Sergio was a clusterfuck. He mixed up dates, shuffled paperwork around, and spoke like a dictim (a dictim is someone who acts like a dick, traumatizes the entire family, then plays the victim).

The clerk did not issue a criminal complaint. I was free to eat my support cookies by 10:00 a.m.

My attorney offered one last piece of advice before we left that morning. He said, "If any of your friends or family are planning to protest Sergio's wedding tomorrow, tell them not to—that's the advice I'm giving you." I smiled, said goodbye, thanked him for kicking Sergio's ass, and we started walking back to our car. I sent out a few text messages letting friends and family know my hearing went great.

As soon as we arrived in Worcester, my parents asked me, "Hey, what time is the pedophile protest tomorrow in Barre?" I told them I was pleading the fifth on this Cinco de Full Moon.

Because I Shake the Tree

At the beginning of June 2023, my brother and his family came up to Massachusetts to visit. A few days before he arrived, he called me to chat. He said his wife, Amy, was flying to the East Coast before him and the kids to attend a few work meetings. Then they would spend some time with Amy's family in New Jersey before taking the train up to Worcester. He asked me what my plans were that week so we could all hang out.

"I don't really have anything planned aside from visiting Vinni and going to Livi's softball games. My life explodes unexpectedly these days, so I really don't plan that much."

"That's fine!" Mikey responded. "What time do the girls get home from school? Maybe we could come by after the bus and hang out. And we would love to go to one of Livi's games! Is there any way we could visit Vinni too, while we're here?"

"I wish you guys could! He would love to see you, Amy, and the kids. Unfortunately, they do not allow visits from extended family, just us and Mom and Dad. I think technically grandparents aren't supposed to visit if they don't live in the home, but I sort of just signed them up for visits the first day he got there, and no one stopped it. The girls get home around 2:45 p.m. so come by whenever after school! Liv has a game this Thursday. I'll be a little late because I have my monthly parenting support group, but we will all be there."

The Arizona crew came over to my house on a Wednesday. It was a beautiful day, weather-wise. Mike, Amy, and I sat out on the patio set in the backyard. The kids excitedly reunited after not seeing each other for about a year. The only thing that made me sad was that Vinni could not be there.

Luna came bursting through the back door, out into the yard, and announced, "Mom! The doorbell just rang!" I immediately froze. Were the police here again?

"Can you see out the window who it is?" I asked her.

"It's cookies from Crumbl!" Luna shouted with joy. I almost burst into happy tears right there. Amy ordered a cookie delivery for us to have after dinner that night. There have been so many times when the darkness and pain is so overwhelming

I can't even function. Then there are times like these—when a simple, surprise cookie delivery lovingly overfills my cup and stomach.

Living in the "Florida of the Southwest," as I jokingly refer to their home state, they don't have access to the best seafood. My mom always makes it a point to serve her daughter-in-law a proper New England clam bake, packed with lobsters, clams, and tons of butter. We chose Friday to be the family lobster night. I would go visit Vinni at five while Felipe and the girls hung out at my mom's, with the rest of our family. My dad said to text him when I leave Vinni's place, so my lobster would be nice and fresh when I got there.

How many lobsters do you think an adult who is smaller than a fifth grader can eat? There is this restaurant called Nordic Lodge that serves unlimited lobsters, steak—basically any type of food you can imagine for a pricey buffet. My cousin Kirsten and I had a contest to see who could eat the most lobsters. I ate six in total, so she choked down a seventh to beat me. We both were sick afterward from overdosing on butter.

When I got to Vinni's place for our visit, the staff told me they were all going to the movies that night, so we should keep an eye on the time so Vinni didn't miss it. This visit was just me and Vinni. I love visits like this, when I can spend one-on-one time with my baby without any added pressure or distractions. I know he appreciates this quality time too.

He has been working with his therapist, Alyssa, for about a month now. She is wonderful! Finally Vinni has a therapist he loves, and he's slowly starting to open up more. In the past, Vinni did not like talking about Sergio, but now he will sporadically say things like, "But Mom, why are some people like Sergio? Like why would an adult want to sexually abuse a kid?" The wheels are always turning in this child's head, and he is smart enough to make sense of almost anything.

I am so happy he is releasing these toxic thoughts. Talking helps. His release comes with a trauma jolt for me, however. Each new detail he shares with me stabs me everywhere in my body as he confirms the horrific trauma his little body had to endure. This Friday we had a short visit so he didn't miss the movie, and it was a happy one overall, but he told me some things. Things that increase the severity of his case. New evidence for the police to investigate.

I emailed my lawyer before I even drove out of Vinni's place. I told him the details that Vinni shared and asked his advice on what to do. He said, "Send an email to the prosecutor saying Vinni disclosed important new details regarding his case and ask how she would like it reported." I thanked him and fired an email off to the DA and my victim-witness advocate. I couldn't go to lobster night though. This trauma jolt of new information was more than enough to make me retreat. I called Felipe and told him I was going straight home. I couldn't act normal and happy and social that night. I needed to watch crime shows in my bed with my cats and draw flowers. I do this instead of going to work a lot, which sucks for my clients—sorry about that! But I have to cope with frequent explosions I can't control. I can control how I comfort myself, which is good and bad sometimes. I may have some unhealthy coping skills, but they aren't the worst. McDonalds, Starbucks, Crumbl cookies, Cadbury mini eggs, macarons from Ivy's Macs—these are my drugs of choice.

That Monday I received a response from my victim-witness advocate. She instructed me, "It would be best to have the detective write a report." Perfect. I emailed the detective on our case asking if he would be able to meet with me that week.

His response was, "Erin, once your son is in a better place, I will be more than willing to take a statement from him. Please let me know when he will be available to come into the police station to give me his new account and share any new evidence with me." I reached out to my lawyer, sharing this response and I was like what the fuck?! We will all be in a better place if you arrest this fuckface monster!

My lawyer told me to send an email just to the prosecutor with the actual details Vinni disclosed. So, I did. I composed the most graphic email I've ever written in my life and sent it to the DA assigned to my case. I closed my email with, "I'm not sure when Vinni will be able to go to the police station, but this was the stuff I wanted documented."

The DA's response concurred with the detective, not my attorney's advice. She said, "Hi Erin, this is information that needs to be documented through an additional interview with Vinni when he is ready to talk about it. Any new information that can be considered needs to come from Vinni and further investigation. I have copied your victim-witness advocate and detective on here so that they are aware. We can reach out to you sometime on Wednesday as I will be unavailable tomorrow."

What's a mom like me to do when nobody wants to do their fucking job? I went completely batshit crazy and emailed a bunch of people, screaming at the top of my lungs, "What in the actual fuck is going on?!" I emailed DMH, the prior hospital Vinni was admitted to, the commissioner of DCF, the executive director of MACA, the school counselor, Vinni's current therapist, and the chief's office at WPD.

I also emailed my attorney again. "In February 2022 when I reported Mia in the room and the cell phone stuff, the detective completely blew me off. I followed up with the DA's office repeatedly and got nowhere. It was never ever mentioned to me that Vinni should come to WPD to be questioned directly by police. But now that's the rule. Is this factual? That all evidence must be communicated directly from the traumatized child to the asshole detective?"

Have I mentioned I love my attorney? Well, I do. He responded with, "Hey Erin—sorry this is happening. It's not a rule, but new information won't be admissible at trial unless Vinni can testify in court to it. Does that mean the police or DA shouldn't know about it unless a nine-year-old is prepared to walk into a police station? Not in my opinion. I think part of this reluctance to take a report from you is the DA and police wanting to not do extra work unless they know Vinni will testify in court."

Everything became crystal clear. It's never been me or that we weren't properly reporting the truth to the authorities. The system doesn't provide justice to victims, the system takes on cases they think they will win.

I responded to my lawyer, "Thank you. I'm going to have a conversation with Vinni about what we should do. And I spoke to a publisher today about my book. At this point, we need a million dollars and a Martha's Vineyard house. We need healing, and the beach will heal us. Fuck Sergio. Get him in jail for any amount of time—great. Create a legacy of suffering for him with my words—it's exactly what he deserves, and the system can't give it to us."

My caseworker from the Department of Mental Health visited my house that day to discuss Vinni's discharge plan. She was a breath of fresh air after speaking to the DA that morning. She said, "Colleen and Carly are working on that legal stuff, but I am here for Vinni, for the clinical side of things. I brought extra release forms for you to sign so we can obtain any police reports we might need."

I can't make the system prosecute Sergio to the fullest, but my DA did essentially triple dog dare me to fuck it up royally—she said loud and clear numerous times, "It's moms like you who will change the system." I think she also said I should get involved in politics to change laws, but fuck that shit—I am no politician.

I'm just a mom shaking the tree, ridding my family of toxicity.

Rotten fruit is falling down,
Because I shake the tree.
If you hurt my babies,
I will fuck you up times three.

Not with my fist, not with a gun,
I pierce your insides with my tongue.
I shake the tree to make you fall,
Like a toxic cannonball.
Into the dirt, forever mute,
No one misses rotten fruit.

The End

I started writing this book last summer, a few weeks after Trevor moved out, just a few days before our therapy kittens came home. Writing about my life as it was unfolding helped me process everything as it was happening. Re-reading my work after the fact was a necessary reminder of everything we have already endured.

Publishing this book provides me with the peace I need to release myself from a system structured to hurt me. It also gives closure to the rotten fruit decomposing at my feet.

The End

With every death, new life flourishes among us.
First falls the rotten fruit, then grows the fungus.

To mom

From
Livi

About the Author

Erin Arvizu is an accountant turned advocate, driven by a fierce love for her family and an unwavering commitment to justice. When her child bravely revealed a dark secret in 2021, writing became Erin's lifeline, providing solace and a platform to expose the flaws of a broken justice system.

Standing at 4'11" tall, she defies expectations with her resolute voice and unyielding spirit. Erin believes in fearlessly fighting for what's right and inspiring others to never give up in the face of adversity.